Sunni and Shī'ah Perspectives on Islām

نظرة أهل السنة والشيعة إلى الإسلام

Dr. Aḥmad 'Abdullāh Salāmah

King Fahd National Library Cataloging-in-Publication Data

Salamah, Ahmad Abdullah
Sunni and Shi'ah Perspectives on Islam – Riyadh
138 p., 14 x 21 cm
ISBN 9960-792-73-0
1 – Islam–General Principles 2 – Shiah (Islamic Sector)
I – Title

211 dc 2550/19

Legal Deposit no. 2550/19
ISBN: 9960-792-73-0

ABUL-QASIM PUBLISHING HOUSE
Telephone (966) 2 671-4793 – Fax (966) 2 672-5523
P.O. Box 6156
Jeddah 21442, Saudi Arabia

THIS BOOK HAS BEEN PRODUCED IN COLLABORATION WITH
ṢAḤEEḤ INTERNATIONAL
Professional Editing and Typesetting of Islamic Literature

Printed and bound in Saudi Arabia at
AL-AMAL ELECTRONIC PRINTERS, JEDDAH
Telephone (966) 2 682-4709 - Fax (966) 2 691-6252

TABLE OF CONTENTS

FOREWORD

The religious beliefs and practices of Shī'ahs distinguish and separate them from the entire Muslim *ummah.* The Shī'ahs have specific beliefs about the attributes of Allāh, the attributes of Allāh's messengers, the position and mission of Prophet Muḥammad (ﷺ), and the authenticity of the Qur'ān. They even have their own unique moral codes. Unfortunately, because of their clannish nature and secretive doctrines, very few people have proper knowledge of their beliefs and practices.

Since its inception Shī'ism has been shrouded in mystery. The initial preaching and propagation of Shī'ism was done only through word of mouth. None of the twelve Shī'ah *imāms* left any documentary evidence of their teachings. It is strange that the Shī'ahs claim to follow Ja'farī *fiqh* when, in fact, Imām Ja'far (may Allāh be pleased with him) did not leave any evidence of having compiled *fiqh* rulings. And later, when the Shī'ahs did start writing about their beliefs, such writings were meant only for Shī'ahs – Sunnis[1] had no access to them. In these writings, sayings attributed to the twelve *imāms* are classified as "*ḥadīth,*" thus eliminating any differentiation between them and the sayings of the Prophet (ﷺ).

Contrary to universal teachings of monotheistic religion, the Shī'ah doctrine of *taqiyyah*[2] teaches its followers to conceal their faith and to hide their beliefs. The following two so-called "*ḥadīths,*" said to have been narrated by the sixth Shī'ah *imām,* Ja'far aṣ-Ṣādiq, clearly elaborate this point:

> "One who exposes something from our religion
> is like one who intentionally kills us."[3]

---

[1] Throughout this book the term "Sunni" has been used in reference to the majority of Muslims, who follow the *sunnah* (way) of the Prophet (ﷺ) as conveyed by his *ṣaḥābah* (companions).

[2] i.e., caution, prudence or dissimulation.

[3] *Uṣūl al-Kāfī,* p. 88.

> "You belong to a religion that whoever conceals it – Allāh will honor him; whoever reveals it – Allāh will disgrace and humiliate him."[4]

Additionally, the practice of *taqiyyah* encourages Shī'ahs to put up a hypocritical front and act in such a way that others will never be exposed to real Shī'ism. It even allows them to lie when the intention is to conceal their religion from non-Shī'ahs. The following Shī'ah narrations testify clearly to this effect:

> Imām Ja'far aṣ-Ṣādiq said: "Associate with your opponents outwardly and oppose them inwardly."[5]

> Zarārah narrated: "I asked a certain question of Imām al-Bāqir, and he gave me its answer. Another person then asked the same question, and the *imām* gave him a different answer. Later, a third person asked the same question, but the *imām's* answer that time was different than the previous two answers. I then asked him, 'O son[6] of the Messenger, the two persons who just came here to ask you questions were from Iraq and were Shī'ahs, yet you gave them contradictory answers.' The *imām* then answered, 'O Zarārah, this is good for me as well as for you, and this will help us survive and prosper.'"[7]

Because of this doctrine neither the Muslim *ummah* nor western scholars have had much genuine and reliable knowledge

---

[4]Ibid., p. 522.
[5]Ibid., p. 244.
[6]i.e., descendant.
[7]Ibid., p. 37.

about Shī'ah beliefs and practices until fairly recently. Many of the declared Shī'ah beliefs revolve around the concept of imamate, the superiority of 'Alī (may Allāh be pleased with him), and the so-called love for the Prophet's family members. Their own love and respect for the Prophet's family, including the noble 'Alī, has led a number of Sunnis to overlook major aspects of their beliefs and accept the Shī'ahs as an integral part of the Muslim *ummah.*

The fact remains, however, that under the pretense of reverence for the Prophet's family members, Shī'ahs have literally evolved an entirely new religion. They have grossly distorted the teachings of the Holy Qur'ān, and completely rejected the sanctity of the authentic *sunnah.* In elevating the sayings of their *imāms* to the rank of the Prophet's sayings, they have classified them as *ḥadīth.* For all practical purposes they reject the authentic sayings of the Prophet (ﷺ) and base their religion on the so-called *ḥadīths* attributed to their *imāms.* Hence, they have rejected one of the most fundamental principles of Islām, which is that Islāmic law can be derived only from the *sunnah* of the Prophet (ﷺ).

Shī'ah scholars are not consistent in their stated faith and beliefs. Consequently, Shī'ism has become subdivided into numerous sub-sects, each having its own *imāms,* whose preachings and personal attributes are often diagonally opposed to each other. The dominant Shī'ah sect, which believes that there was a total of twelve *imāms,* is known as *al-ithnā 'ashriyyah,* meaning in Arabic, "twelvers." This book deals mainly with the beliefs and practices of this Shī'ah sect.

The following pages present an objective analysis of Shī'ah beliefs, doctrines and practices, which have been assessed and evaluated from the standpoint of Qur'ānic teachings and the *ḥadīth* of the Prophet (ﷺ). Judgement is left with the reader to decide whether or not Shī'ah beliefs and practices can stand this test. The following will help readers to understand and judge the matter in an unbiased manner:

- While presenting the Shī'ah point of view, this book gives an exhaustive account of all the arguments used by the Shī'ahs in support of their beliefs. These consist of evidences from the Qur'ān, prophetic *ḥadīth,* the sayings of their *imāms,* and Islāmic history which Shī'ah scholars have used in support of their belief.
- Only Shī'ah sources, which are considered to be the most original and reliable by the Shī'ahs themselves, have been utilized to present the Shī'ah point of view.
- Every Shī'ah argument has been presented verbatim as it appears in the Shī'ah source. No deletion or addition has been made in any of the quotations.

Each Shī'ah position is accompanied by the Sunni perspective on the same issue, where evidences are taken mostly from the Qur'ān and sometimes from the Prophet's *ḥadīth.*

Separate annotated bibliographies have been presented for Shī'ah and Sunni sources at the end of this book.

Dr. Aḥmad 'Abdullāh Salāmah
Jeddah, Saudi Arabia

CALIPHATE VS. IMAMATE

One of the fundamental differences between the Sunnis and Shī'ahs concerns the issue of caliphate versus imamate. Sunnis believe in the validity of the elected caliphs, who were vested with leadership of the *ummah* after the demise of the Prophet (ﷺ). Shī'ahs believe that there were divinely designated *imāms* and consider the caliphs usurpers of the rights of *imāms.*

The fundamental difference between the Sunnis and Shī'ahs is not so much in the usage of the terms "caliph" or "*imām*" but in the total concept of caliphate and imamate. For Sunnis, the belief in caliphate is neither an essential nor a recommended part of the faith. When a person declares himself to be a believer, he only needs to testify: "I bear witness that there is no god but Allāh and that Muḥammad is His servant and His messenger."

But for Shī'ahs, belief in imamate is an integral and the most preferred part of faith. One's faith is accepted and complete only when he testifies: "I bear witness that there is no god but Allāh and that Muḥammad is His servant and His messenger and that 'Alī is the designated *imām* and trustee of Allāh."

The difference is further evident in the *adhān*[1] preceding congregational prayer in a Muslim society. It proclaims that there is no god but Allāh and that Muḥammad (ﷺ) is Allāh's Messenger. But the Shī'ah *mu'adhdhin* (caller) adds certain words not present in the original *adhān,* which are: "and 'Alī is the trustee and the nominated caliph of the Prophet, without anyone between them." Thus, next to belief in Allāh and the prophethood of Muḥammad (ﷺ), the belief in the designated succession of 'Alī is declared a part of the Shī'ah creed. The Sunnis point out that there is not a single verse in the Qur'ān that calls for belief in imamate. Thus, the first fundamental

[1]The call to prayer.

difference between the two groups is in the very definition of a Muslim and what he believes.

The second fundamental difference is in the concept of prophethood and the noble mission of Muḥammad (ﷺ):

﴿الْيَوْمَ أَكْمَلْتُ لَكُمْ دِينَكُمْ وَأَتْمَمْتُ عَلَيْكُمْ نِعْمَتِي وَرَضِيتُ لَكُمُ الإِسْلاَمَ دِينًا﴾

"This day I have perfected for you your religion and completed My favor upon you and have approved of Islām for you as a religion."[2]

This verse was revealed on the ninth of Dhul-Ḥijjah, 10 A.H., when the Prophet (ﷺ) delivered his famous *Farewell Address.* Muslim historians and Qur'ānic commentators also recorded that when the Prophet (ﷺ) recited these verses, Abū Bakr wept. People around him said that the verse declared the completion of Allāh's blessings. Abū Bakr replied that it also meant that the Prophet (ﷺ) had completed his mission and would not remain among them much longer. This proved to be true, and the Prophet (ﷺ) died soon after.

Shī'ah commentators on the Qur'ān give a unique explanation for the aforementioned verses. They assert that when the Prophet (ﷺ) was returning from his last pilgrimage and stopped at a place called Ghadeer Khumm, the Archangel Gabriel brought this command to him:

﴿يَا أَيُّهَا الرَّسُولُ بَلِّغْ مَا أُنزِلَ إِلَيْكَ مِن رَّبِّكَ وَإِن لَّمْ تَفْعَلْ فَمَا بَلَّغْتَ رِسَالَتَهُ وَاللهُ يَعْصِمُكَ مِنَ النَّاسِ﴾

"O Messenger, announce that which has been revealed to you from your Lord, and if you do not, then you have not conveyed His message. And Allāh will protect you from the people."[3]

---

[2] *Sūrah al-Mā'idah,* 5:3.
[3] *Sūrah al-Mā'idah,* 5:67.

At that, they say, the Prophet (ﷺ) ordered the men to halt and assemble. He then proclaimed that 'Alī was his brother, his successor and the *imām* after him. Immediately thereafter, Allāh revealed:

﴿اليَومَ أَكمَلتُ لَكُم دِينَكُم وَأَتمَمتُ عَلَيكُم نِعمَتِي وَرَضِيتُ لَكُمُ الإِسلامَ دِيناً﴾

"This day I have perfected for you your religion and completed My favor upon you and have approved of Islām for you as a religion."[4]

According to Shī'ahs, it was 'Alī's nomination to the imamate that completed Allāh's blessings upon the believers and made Islām acceptable to Allāh. Accordingly, the mission and the institution of prophethood would have been incomplete unless associated with and supplemented by the imamate of 'Alī. Sunnis, on the contrary, reject this interpretation and consider that the prophethood is an independent and perfect institution not contingent upon the belief in imamate.

THE SUNNI CONCEPT OF CALIPHATE

The Arabic term "*khalīfah*" means "successor" or "deputy." Thus, a caliph, in his personal capacity, is not a sovereign but only represents the true sovereign who is none other than Allāh, the Almighty. Consequently, exercising his powers, he cannot transgress the limits of his role set by Allāh. Should he do so, he would render himself liable to be removed from office.

The office of caliphate is not reserved for a certain family, nor do family connections have anything to do with this office. Once a caliph passes away, his office is not automatically transmitted to his son. The Muslim *ummah* must always choose a new caliph, as was the case in the choice of Abū Bakr, 'Umar, 'Uthmān and 'Alī.

---

[4] *Sūrah al-Mā'idah,* 5:3.

A person cannot himself aspire to be the caliph. Through mutual consultation the *ummah* may confer this office upon any qualified Muslim, the primary considerations being personal integrity, piety, ability, and sound knowledge and practice of the Qur'ān and *sunnah.* The caliph must conduct his affairs by mutual consultation, and other individuals have the right to agree or disagree with him.

A caliph is a mortal human being with no supernatural powers or attributes. The caliphate was a political system, not an integral or preferred part of one's faith. The following verses of the Qur'ān support this view:

﴿إِنَّ أَكرَمَكُم عِندَ اللهِ أَتقَاكُم﴾

"Indeed, the most noble of you in the sight of Allāh is the most righteous."[5]

﴿وَعَدَ اللهُ الَّذِينَ آمَنُوا مِنكُم وَعَمِلُوا الصَّالِحَاتِ لَيَستَخلِفَنَّهُم فِي الأَرضِ كَمَا استَخلَفَ الَّذِينَ مِن قَبلِهِم﴾

"Allāh has promised those who have believed among you and done righteous deeds that He will surely grant them succession [to authority] upon the earth just as He granted it to those before them."[6]

These verses highlight some of the salient features of the caliphate as opposed to imamate. A detailed presentation of what the Qur'ān and *ḥadīth* say about caliphate will be discussed in a later section.

THE SHĪ'AH CONCEPT OF IMAMATE

The Arabic term "*imām*" means "leader" but carries a very special connotation in Shī'ah beliefs. This can be summarized as follows:

---

[5] *Sūrah al-Ḥujurāt,* 49:13.

[6] *Sūrah an-Nūr,* 24:55.

- The *imām* is designated by Allāh. Individuals have no freedom in the choice or election of an *imām.*
- The institution of imamate was reserved for 'Alī and his male progeny through Fāṭimah. Thus, when an *imām* dies, authority is automatically transferred to his eldest son.
- The *imāms* are considered infallible and divinely protected from all sin and human weakness.
- They are not seen as ordinary human beings but as equal in rank to the prophets in their attributes and their mission.

The belief in imamate is an integral and most important part of the Shī'ah faith. The following saying, attributed to the fifth Shī'ah *imām,* al-Bāqir testifies to this effect:

> "Islām is based on five pillars: prayer, fasting, pilgrimage, *zakāh* and imamate. Of these, the most important and preferred one is the belief in imamate."[7]

This belief is common among all Shī'ahs. Various Shī'ah sub-sects, however, differ over the sequence and the number of their *imāms. Al-ithnā 'ashriyyah,* the dominant Shī'ah sect, believes there were a total of twelve *imāms.* The twelfth *imām* did not die but only disappeared, and now rules the world and guides the *ummah* in absentia. He will reappear before the Day of Judgement and proclaim his leadership.

Although Shī'ahs make these claims, they do not give any valid evidences from the Qur'ān in support of them. All verses quoted in Shī'ah sources in support of imamate are either incomplete or out of context. For example:

---

[7]In contrast to these, the pillars of faith according to the Prophet's *sunnah* are: testimony to the divinity of Allāh and messengership of Muḥammad (ﷺ), prayer, *zakāh,* fasting and pilgrimage.

﴿إِنِّي جَاعِلُكَ لِلنَّاسِ إِمَامًا﴾

"Indeed, I will make you a leader [imām] for the people."[8]

Shī'ah literature, asserting the concept of imamate, invariably cites this portion of the verse and explains it by adding that the *imām* is always designated by Allāh. The complete verse, however, reads as follows:

﴿وَإِذِ ابْتَلَى إِبْرَاهِيمَ رَبُّهُ بِكَلِمَاتٍ فَأَتَمَّهُنَّ قَالَ إِنِّي جَاعِلُكَ لِلنَّاسِ إِمَامًا قَالَ وَمِن ذُرِّيَّتِي قَالَ لَا يَنَالُ عَهْدِي الظَّالِمِينَ﴾

"And [mention, O Muḥammad], when Abraham was tried by his Lord with words [i.e., commands] and he fulfilled them. [Allāh] said, 'Indeed, I will make you a leader for the people.' [Abraham] said, 'And of my descendants?' [Allāh] said, 'My covenant does not include the wrongdoers.'"[9]

When read as a whole, the verse completely negates the Shī'ah concept of hereditary imamate. It speaks of Abraham, who was a divinely designated prophet and leader of his people.

A second example can be found in this verse:

﴿وَجَعَلْنَاهُمْ أَئِمَّةً يَهْدُونَ بِأَمْرِنَا﴾

"And We made them leaders [imāms], guiding by Our command."[10]

The Shī'ah explanation of this verse is that an *imām* is always inspired and designated by Allāh. Thus, the Muslim *ummah* has no choice in the selection or election of their leaders. Again, Shī'ahs quote the verse without regard for the preceding ones which define the pronoun "them."

---

[8] *Sūrah al-Baqarah,* 2:124.
[9] *Sūrah al-Baqarah,* 2:124.
[10] *Sūrah al-Anbiyā',* 21:73.

﴿وَوَهَبنَا لَهُ إِسحَاقَ وَيَعقُوبَ نَافِلَةً وَكُلاً جَعَلنَا صَالِحِينَ. وَجَعَلنَاهُم أَئِمَّةً يَهدُونَ بِأَمرِنَا وَأَوحَينَا إِلَيهِم فِعلَ الخَيرَاتِ وَإِقَامَ الصَّلاَةِ وَإِيتَاءَ الزَّكَاةِ وَكَانُوا لَنَا عَابِدِينَ﴾

"And We gave him [i.e., Abraham] Isaac and Jacob in addition, and each [of them] We made righteous. And We made them leaders, guiding by Our command. And We inspired to them the doing of good deeds, establishment of prayer, and giving of zakāh; and they were worshippers of Us."[11]

These two verses speak again of prophets, who were divinely appointed. But Shī'ahs quote only the portion which they associate with their *imāms.*

THE SPECIAL ATTRIBUTES OF SHĪ'AH IMĀMS

Since Shī'ah *imāms* are said to be divinely designated, they must possess special attributes and powers. One who believes in the concept of imamate also believes in unique attributes of the *imāms.* Following are a few quotations concerning their attributes from what are regarded as original sources of Shī'ah beliefs and practices.

◆ The Infallibility of the Imāms

1. All twelve *imāms* are infallible and absolutely immune from sin. They never (in their lives) committed any wrongs.[12]
2. All the *imāms* are infallible just like the prophets. The Shī'ahs derive their religion from their immaculate *imāms.*[13]

---

[11] *Sūrah al-Anbiyā'*, 21:72-73.
[12] *Minhāj al-Kirāmah,* pp. 32-33.
[13] Ibid., p. 22.

◆ The Extraordinary Knowledge of the Imāms

1. By listening to the voice of a person, the *imāms* knew if that person was destined to go to Hell or to Heaven. They would thus answer his questions accordingly.[14]
2. It is narrated by Abū Baṣeer that Imām Ja'far aṣ-Ṣādiq, the sixth Shī'ah *imām* said: "If a man [i.e., the *imām*] does not know what will reach him [in a day] and what he will face [in the future], he cannot be regarded an authority for the believers."[15]
3. The *imāms* have knowledge of the time of their death, and they choose the time of their death.[16]
4. The narrator says, "I asked Imām ar-Ridhā[17] (the eighth Shī'ah *imām*) to pray for my family and me. The *imām* answered, 'I cannot do that since all your deeds are being presented to me every day in the morning and evening.'"[18]

It appears from the above citations that Shī'ah *imāms* in their boundless knowledge of the unseen have surpassed the knowledge of the Prophet (ﷺ), which, as stated by Allāh in the Qur'ān, is limited:

﴿قُل لا أَقُولُ لَكُم عِندِي خزَائِنُ اللهِ وَلا أَعلَمُ الغَيبَ وَلا أَقُولُ لَكُم إِنّي مَلَكٌ إِن أَتَّبِعُ إِلاَّ مَا يُوحى إِلَيَّ﴾

"Say, [O Muḥammad], 'I do not tell you that I have the depositories [of the treasures] of Allāh nor that I know the unseen, nor do I tell you that I am an angel. I only follow what is revealed to me.'"[19]

---

14 *Uṣūl al-Kāfī,* p. 185.
15 Ibid.
16 Ibid.
17 Commonly spelled "Reza" or "Raza."
18 *Uṣūl al-Kāfī,* p. 253.
19 *Sūrah al-An'ām,* 6:50.

◆ Imamate Versus Prophethood

1. It is narrated by Zayd Shamān that he heard Imām Ja'far aṣ-Ṣādiq say: "Allāh first made Abraham His servant, then His messenger, then His prophet, then His friend. After making him His friend, He made him an *imām*."[20]
2. The truth is that in matters of their relative merits and essential qualities and all those attributes that count for excellence, there is no difference, whatsoever, between a prophet and an *imām*.[21]
3. The narrator says that he heard from Imām Ja'far aṣ-Ṣādiq, "The *imāms* are like prophets, but they are not prophets. They are not allowed to have as many wives as the prophets; otherwise, they share all the attributes and virtues given to the prophets."[22]

◆ Infallibility is Part of Imamate but Not of Prophethood

1. Imām Ja'far aṣ-Ṣādiq said: "There are three foundations of *kufr* [disbelief]: greed, pride and jealousy. [Prophet] Ādam committed an act of greed. He was forbidden [to eat] from the tree, but greed motivated him to eat. Satan committed an act of pride. When he was asked to bow before Ādam, he refused. Ādam's sons committed an act of jealousy when one of them killed the other."[23]
2. Allāh asked Ādam not to be jealous of the Prophet's family members. Allāh said to Ādam, "Do not look with jealousy towards my beloved ones, lest you be deprived of My blessings and be disgraced," but Ādam did not stop envying them. Thus, Ādam and Eve were expelled from Heaven as a punishment.[24]

---

20 *Uṣūl al-Kāfī,* p. 203.
21 *Ḥayāt al-Qulūb,* vol. 3, p. 3.
22 *Uṣūl al-Kāfī,* p. 310.
23 Ibid., p. 517.
24 *Ḥayāt al-Qulūb,* vol. 1, p. 50.

3. The following is a "*ḥadīth*" from Imām ar-Ridhā: "The characteristics of prophets are [merely] to keep their bodies clean, use perfume, have frequent sexual intercourse, and keep many women."[25]

Thus, in glorification of their *imāms,* Shī'ahs even go to the extent of degrading the prophets.

◆ The Boundless Power of the Imāms

1. Imām ar-Ridhā said: "Allāh created us in the best of stature and gave us the best of faces. He made us trustees of the earth and the heavens. We talk [even] to the trees. Allāh is worshipped because of our prayers. If we were not present, Allāh will not be worshipped."[26]
2. The *imām* occupies such distinguished position and elevated rank and commands such authority that each and every particle of the universe surrenders to his will and submits to his authority.[27]
3. "One of the basic and essential beliefs of our religion is that the *imāms* occupy such [distinguished] position that the most honored angels and prophets cannot reach it."[28]

◆ The Unique Attributes of 'Alī

The previous quotations present but a few general characteristics attributed to all Shī'ah *imāms.* 'Alī, being the first *imām,*[29] is said to have possessed a number of additional

---

[25]Ibid., vol. 1, p. 21.

[26]*Uṣūl al-Kāfī,* p. 221.

[27]*Al-Ḥukūmah al-Islamiyyah,* p. 52.

[28]Ibid., p. 52.

[29]Neither 'Alī nor his direct descendants considered themselves anything but Muslims and certainly not propagators of any sect or separate religious creed. It is the Shī'ahs who consider them as their own religious leaders, attributing to them many inconceivable narrations to support their doctrines.

attributes. Shī'ah commentaries give the impression that the Qur'ān was revealed to glorify the name of 'Alī and that the only mission of the Prophet (ﷺ) was to establish the imamate of 'Alī. The following Shī'ah citations assert 'Alī's unique attributes:[30]

1. Imām al-Bāqir said: "'Alī was *muḥaddath,* that is, the angels used to talk to him."[31]
2. The narrator said that he heard 'Alī say: "We are Allāh's eyes, His hands, His sides and His gateway."[32]
3. After the Prophet (ﷺ), 'Alī has the same rights of obedience and respect as the Prophet (ﷺ). This is also true of all successive *imāms.*[33]
4. It is narrated that Abū 'Abdullāh [i.e., Imām Ja'far] said: "I do whatever was brought by 'Alī and refrain from whatever was forbidden by him. He has the same superiority of rank as the Prophet (ﷺ) himself."[34]
5. 'Alī said: "I am the one in whose command Allāh has put the clouds, lightening, thunder, darkness, rivers, mountains, stars, moon and the sun. I am the leader and the guide of this *ummah.*"[35]

These so-called *ḥadīths* give Shī'ah *imāms* a position equal to or higher than that of the angels and prophets, including Prophet Muḥammad (ﷺ). This leads one to four basic questions:

1. If, as they claim, the *imām* was divinely appointed to lead the Muslim *ummah* and belief in imamate was intended to be the most essential and preferred part of a believer's

---

[30]For a further discussion of this subject, see "The Superiority of 'Alī," p. 42.
[31] *Uṣūl al-Kāfī,* p. 308.
[32]Ibid., p. 309.
[33]Ibid., pp. 118-119.
[34]Ibid., pp. 165-66.
[35] *Ḥayāt al-Qulūb,* p. 436.

faith, why did Allāh not reveal that in His Book? Muslim scholars have not found a single mention in any verse about imamate in the Qur'ān.[36]

2. Since the attributes and merits of the Shī'ah *imāms,* according to the above-mentioned *ḥadīths,* supersede those of Allāh's honored angels and chosen prophets, should one believe that Shī'ah *imāms* are infallible and superior to the angels and prophets or reject these Shī'ah *ḥadīths* as baseless concoctions?
3. The claims attributed to 'Alī about his infinite powers, boundless knowledge and unique attributes give him a position superior even to that of the Prophet (ﷺ). No book of history or *ḥadīth* has recorded that Prophet Muḥammad (ﷺ) ever made a claim to the unique attributes supposedly possessed by 'Alī. Can one then accept the position that the Shī'ah *imām* in rank and merit was superior to the Prophet (ﷺ), or must he reject the sources of Shī'ah *ḥadīth*?
4. If Shī'ah *imāms* possessed such special powers and unique attributes, why was each of them unsuccessful in his role and mission? All of them failed to have any authority over the Muslim *ummah* and lived isolated lives. Early Muslim history recorded a total of sixty-five different persons who claimed to be divinely designated *imāms,* revolted against existing governments, fought for their claims and were ultimately killed. On the contrary, history witnessed the marvelous success of the Prophet's mission at the hands of the four Rightly Guided Caliphs.

---

[36]It has been confirmed historically that the Qur'ān in widespread use among Muslims today is the same original words that were revealed to Prophet Muḥammad (ﷺ), unchanged and unaltered. Shī'ah accusations that it has been tampered with appeared in their commentaries and writings, but no one has come out with a Shī'ah version. They claim that the true Qur'ān disappeared along with al-Mahdī, the awaited *imām,* and there is no consensus among their scholars as to what it contained.

These questions remain unanswered and pose a challenge to Shīʻah belief in the superiority of ʻAlī and the alleged attributes of divinely nominated *imāms.*

The reliability and validity of the various arguments for the right of ʻAlī and his descendants to the imamate of the *ummah* will now be discussed. The Shīʻah point of view will be presented first, followed by the Sunni answer to each of the arguments.

SHĪʻAH ARGUMENTS IN FAVOR OF THE IMAMATE

1. The Verse of Purity

The "verse of purity" is a widely quoted Shīʻah argument in support of ʻAlī's right to succession and the infallibility of Shīʻah *imāms*:

﴿إِنَّمَا يُرِيدُ اللهُ لِيُذهِبَ عَنكُمُ الرِّجسَ أهـلَ البَيتِ وَيُطَهِّرَكُم تَطهِيرًا﴾

> *"Allāh wants only to remove from you the impurity [of sin], O people of the [Prophet's] household, and to purify you with [extensive] purification."*[37]

When this verse was revealed, the Prophet (ﷺ) assembled his daughter Fāṭimah, her sons al-Ḥasan and al-Ḥusayn, and his cousin ʻAlī. He then covered the four including himself with his mantle and, invoking Allāh, said, "O Allāh, these are my household. Keep them away from every kind of impurity, purified with perfect purification." Witnessing this marvelous occasion, the Prophet's wife Umm Salamah humbly submitted, "O Prophet of Allāh, may I also join the group?" The Prophet (ﷺ) replied, "Remain in your place, for you are [already] in a good state." Thus, only five persons are included: the Prophet

[37] *Sūrah al-Aḥzāb,* 33:33.

(ﷺ), ‘Alī, Fāṭimah, al-Ḥasan and al-Ḥusayn. Moreover, by virtue of the Prophet's supplication, they were purified from all sins. Consequently, ‘Alī and his descendants are infallible and superior to the rest of the Muslim *ummah* and thus entitled to be the *imāms* or leaders of the Muslim *ummah.*[38]

The True Meaning of "Ahl al-Bayt"

The words "*ahl al-bayt*" appear in the second half of verse thirty-three in *Sūrah al-Aḥzāb.* The relevant verses constitute a self-contained section from verse twenty-eight to thirty-four:

﴿يَا أَيُّهَا النَّبِيُّ قُلْ لِأَزْوَاجِكَ إِن كُنتُنَّ تُرِدْنَ الحَيَاةَ الدُّنيَا وَزِينَتَهَا فَتَعَالَيْنَ أُمَتِّعْكُنَّ وَأُسَرِّحْكُنَّ سَرَاحًا جَمِيلاً. وَإِن كُنتُنَّ تُرِدْنَ اللهَ وَرَسُولَهُ وَالدَّارَ الأَخِرَةَ فَإِنَّ اللهَ أَعَدَّ لِلمُحسِنَاتِ مِنكُنَّ أَجرًا عَظِيمًا. يَانِسَاءَ النَّبِيِّ مَن يَأتِ مِنكُنَّ بِفَاحِشَةٍ مُبَيِّنَةٍ يُضَاعَفْ لَهَا العَذَابُ ضِعفَينِ وَكَانَ ذَٰلِكَ عَلَى اللهِ يَسِيرًا. وَمَن يَقنُت مِنكُنَّ لِلَّهِ وَرَسُولِهِ وَتَعمَل صَالِحًا نُؤتِهَا أَجْرَهَا مَرَّتَينِ وَأَعتَدنَا لَهَا رِزقًا كَرِيمًا. يَانِسَاءَ النَّبِيِّ لَستُنَّ كَأَحَدٍ مِنَ النِّسَاءِ إِنِ اتَّقَيتُنَّ فَلا تَخضَعنَ بِالقَولِ فَيَطمَعَ الَّذِي فِي قَلبِهِ مَرَضٌ وَقُلنَ قَولاً مَعرُوفًا. وَقَرْنَ فِي بُيُوتِكُنَّ وَلا تَبَرَّجنَ تَبَرُّجَ الجَاهِلِيَّةِ الأُولَى وَأَقِمنَ الصَّلاةَ وَآتِينَ الزَّكَاةَ وَأَطِعنَ اللهَ وَرَسُولَهُ إِنَّمَا يُرِيدُ اللهُ لِيُذهِبَ عَنكُمُ الرِّجسَ أَهلَ البَيتِ وَيُطَهِّرَكُم تَطهِيرًا. وَاذكُرنَ مَا يُتلَى فِي بُيُوتِكُنَّ مِن آيَاتِ اللهِ وَالحِكمَةِ إِنَّ اللهَ كَانَ لَطِيفًا خَبِيرًا﴾

"O Prophet, say to your wives, If you should desire the worldly life and its adornment, then come, I will provide for you and give you a

---

[38] *Imāmate,* pp. 29-32. In other narrations the wife is specified as ‘Ā’ishah.

gracious release.(28) But if you should desire Allāh and His Messenger and the home of the Hereafter, then indeed, Allāh has prepared for the doers of good among you a great reward.'(29) O wives of the Prophet, whoever of you should commit a clear immorality, for her the punishment would be doubled two fold, and that for Allāh is ever easy.(30) And whoever of you devoutly obeys Allāh and His Messenger and does righteousness, We will give her her reward twice; and We have prepared for her a generous provision.(31) O wives of the Prophet, you are not like anyone among women. If you fear Allāh, then do not be soft in speech [to men],[39] *lest he in whose heart is disease should covet, but speak with appropriate speech.(32) And abide in your houses and do not display yourselves as [was] the display of the former times of ignorance. And establish prayer and give zakāh and obey Allāh and His Messenger. Allāh wants only to remove from you the impurity [of sin], O people of the [Prophet's] household, and to purify you with [extensive] purification.(33) And remember what is recited in your houses of the verses of Allāh and wisdom [i.e., the sunnah]. Indeed, Allāh is ever Subtle and Acquainted [with all things]."(34)*[40]

Verse twenty-eight and twenty-nine are addressed to the Prophet (ﷺ). Verse thirty and thirty-one are explicitly

---

[39]The meaning has also been given as "You are not like any among women if you fear Allāh. So do not be soft in speech..."

[40]*Sūrah al-Aḥzāb,* 33:28-34.

addressed to the Prophet's wives. Verse thirty-two again addresses the Prophet's wives directly and reminds them that they are not like ordinary women.

Then comes verse thirty-three, the widely quoted Shīʻah argument for the infallibility and supremacy of ʻAlī. The first half of the verse says: *"And abide in your houses and do not display yourselves as [was] the display of the former times of ignorance."* It is quiet clear that these words are a continuation of the previous verses which are directly addressed to the Prophets' wives. The second half of the verse then says: *"Allāh intends only to remove from you the impurity [of sin], O people of the [Prophet's] household, and to purify you with [extensive] purification."*

These words show clearly that the whole section is addressed to the Prophet (ﷺ) and his wives. The verbs and pronouns used in the preceding and following verses are feminine in gender. In verse thirty-three, however, the pronouns used after "*ahl al-bayt*" are masculine. This is because in Arabic grammar the masculine gender is used when both males and females are included. Thus, the verses as a whole refer to and include the Prophet's wives. ʻAlī, Fāṭimah and the noble children, al-Ḥasan and al-Ḥusayn by virtue of the Prophet's supplication have also been included among his family members.

The Shīʻahs quote only the second half of verse thirty-three and claim that only those four and not the Prophet's wives constitute the members of the Prophet's family. If the Shīʻah version is accepted and the Prophet's wives are excluded from the term "*ahl al-bayt,*" it would mean that from verse twenty-nine to the clause under discussion, Almighty Allāh: asked the Prophet's wives to choose between this world and the next, warned them of a double punishment in case of unseemly conduct, promised them a double reward if they were virtuous, reminded them to be models of decency and decorum, exhorted them to establish regular prayer and charity and then says that He has enjoined upon them all those things because He wants to remove impurity from ʻAlī, Fāṭimah, al-Ḥasan and al-Ḥusayn! Where is the logic?

The Term "Ahl al-Bayt" in the Qur'ān

Innumerable pages of Shīʻah books are devoted to the argument that the term "*ahl al-bayt*" does not include the Prophet's wives. The reason for this is obvious. If the term "*ahl al-bayt*" included the Prophet's wives, then they too would have been purified of sins like ʻAlī and his descendants. That would negate the Shīʻah myth of ʻAlī's absolute superiority and destroy the foundation of the imamate doctrine. Hence, Shīʻah scholars, historians and commentators on the Qur'ān have produced vast amounts of literature presenting the argument that ʻAlī and descendants are the only legitimate family members and that the Prophet's wives are not included in the term "*ahl al-bayt.*" Therefore, the evidence that "*ahl al-bayt*" in the Qur'ān refers to members of a household, including the wives, must be presented.

The Qur'ān records an incident in the house of Prophet Abraham. When the angels gave him the good news of a son and a grandson, his wife exclaimed, "Shall I bear a child while I am an old woman..." The angels replied:

﴿أَتَعجَبِينَ مِن أَمرِ اللهِ رَحمَةُ اللهِ وَبَرَكَاتُهُ عَلَيكُم أَهلَ البَيتِ﴾

> *"Are you amazed at the decree of Allāh? May the mercy of Allāh and His blessings be upon you, people of the household."*[41]

It is obvious from the use of a feminine verb that the term "*ahl al-bayt*" here refers to and includes Prophet Abraham's wife. There appears to be no reason that the same term used in *Sūrah al-Aḥzāb* would not include the Prophet's wives.

---

[41] *Sūrah Hūd,* 11:73.

It seems relevant here to point out a unique honor bestowed upon the Prophet's wives. In the Qur'ān, Allāh refers to them as "wives of the Prophet," not "wives of Muḥammad," thus associating them with the attributes of prophethood rather than the personality of Muḥammad (ﷺ). In contrast, the wives of other prophets were called "the wife of Noah," "wife of Lot," "wife of Abraham," etc. The Qur'ān thus associates these women with the personalities of the prophets and not the attributes of prophethood. Thus, the Qur'ān bestowed an additional honor upon Prophet Muḥammad's wives.

Furthermore, the Qur'ān clearly states:

﴿يَانِسَاءَ النَّبِيِّ لَسْتُنَّ كَأَحَدٍ مِنَ النِّسَاءِ﴾

"O wives of the Prophet, you are not like anyone among women."[42]

﴿النَّبِيُّ أَولَى بِالْمُؤْمِنِينَ مِن أَنفُسِهِم وَأَزوَاجُهُ أُمَّهَاتُهُم﴾

"The Prophet is more worthy of the believers than one of another, and his wives are their mothers."[43]

Alas! For these noble persons Shī'ahs have nothing but abuse, even going to the extent of denying them their right to being classified as the Prophet's family members.

Returning to the discussion of the "verse of purity," the word "*taṭheer*" needs to be explained. It simply means "purification," and Allāh stated that He wanted to purify the Prophet's family. Shī'ahs explain this as being Allāh's declaration of their infallibility, which they claim applies only to 'Alī, Fāṭimah and their descendants. If the Shī'ah interpretation of the word is accepted, then the Prophet's wives would also be included as "infallible." Additionally, the term

---

[42] *Sūrah al-Aḥzāb*, 33:32.

[43] *Sūrah al-Aḥzāb*, 33:6.

"purification" has been used in connection with the warriors who fought in the battle of Badr.[44] Consequently, all the warriors of Badr should also be classified as "infallible." There were many of the warriors of Badr alive and present at the time of the Prophet's demise. But according to Shī'ah beliefs, all of them gave up Islām and became disbelievers, although the Qur'ān uses the same term, "*taṭheer,*" for them as well. To quote Shī'ah sources:

> "After the death of the Prophet (ﷺ), all his companions except three gave up Islām. They were Miqdād, Abū Dharr and Salmān."[45]

> "There is a narration by Imām al-Bāqir that after the death of the Prophet (ﷺ), all the Prophet's companions except three became disbelievers. They were Salmān, Abū Dharr and Miqdād. He was then asked about 'Ammār. The *imām* said, 'He first denied the truth but accepted it later on.' The *imām* then added, 'If you really want to know the one who never had the slightest doubt about the truth [regarding 'Alī's imamate], it was only Miqdād, since Salmān for a while had doubts.'"[46]

Ḥadīth al-Kisā'

Discussion now returns to the *kisā'* (mantle) incident quoted earlier. After the "verses of purity" were revealed, the Prophet (ﷺ) gathered 'Alī, Fāṭimah, al-Ḥasan and al-Ḥusayn under his mantle and prayed to Allāh to purify them as members of his *ahl bayt.* According to Shī'ahs, 'Alī, Fāṭimah and their descendants are the only legitimate *ahl al-bayt*

---

[44] See *Sūrah al-Anfāl,* 8:11.
[45] *Furu' al-Kāfī,* vol. 2, p. 115.
[46] *Biḥār al-Anwār,* p. 46.

(family members) by virtue of this *ḥadīth,* who have been purified of all of their sins and are thus infallible. This supports 'Alī's right to the imamate and is recorded in Shī'ah books as "*ḥadīth al-kisā'.*" Sunni books of *ḥadīth* also record this incident as previously explained in correlation with verses 28-34 of *Sūrah al-Aḥzāb.* Their scholars have raised the following points:

If *ahl al-bayt* in the "verse of purity" (v. 33) refers only to the above-mentioned four persons, the Prophet (ﷺ) would have known it. Why, then, was it necessary for the Prophet (ﷺ) to collect the four, throw his mantle over them and state that they were his *ahl bayt*? Did he for a moment think that Allāh did not know his *ahl bayt*? Or did he want to confirm his own understanding of *ahl al-bayt*? Moreover, when Allāh had already promised to purify his *ahl bayt,* why did he then make a separate supplication for 'Alī and his family? Did he not have full faith in Allāh's promise? These questions automatically emerge from the Shī'ah interpretation of this *ḥadīth.*

Would it not be more logical and realistic to accept the Sunni interpretation of "*ḥadīth al-kisā',*" which is that since the whole discourse in those verses was addressed to the Prophet's wives, it is they who were primarily specified by the term "*ahl al-bayt.*" This is perhaps the reason that when Umm Salamah requested him to include her, the Prophet (ﷺ) told her, "Remain in your place, you are [already] in a good state." He did, however, make a special supplication for 'Alī, Fāṭimah and their children, so that they would also receive Allāh's blessings and purification.

It should be added that this action of the Prophet (ﷺ) was not limited to 'Alī and his family members. At-Tirmidhī recorded in his book of *ḥadīths*:

> *"It is narrated by al-'Abbās [the Prophet's uncle] that the Prophet (ﷺ) said to him, 'On*

Monday, come to me and bring your sons. I shall make a supplication for you which will benefit you and your sons.' Al-'Abbās said that he and his sons presented themselves before the Prophet (ﷺ), who placed his mantle over them and prayed, 'O Allāh, grant forgiveness to al-'Abbās and his sons and cleanse their hearts so they will not commit sins.'"

If the mantle incident is taken as a declaration of 'Alī's infallibility, then al-'Abbās and his sons could have claimed the same. Thus, it becomes clear that the mantle incident neither excluded the Prophet's wives from his household (*ahl al-bayt*) nor served as a declaration of infallibility for 'Alī and his descendants.

2. The Beggar Incident

Shī'ahs also claim that the following verse from the Qur'ān testifies to the imamate of 'Alī:

﴿إِنَّمَا وَلِيُّكُمُ اللهُ وَرَسُولُهُ وَالَّذِينَ آمَنُوا الَّذِينَ يُقِيمُونَ الصَّلَاةَ وَيُؤْتُونَ الزَّكَاةَ وَهُمْ رَاكِعُونَ﴾

"Your patron is none but Allāh and [therefore] His Messenger and those who have believed – those who establish prayer and give zakāh, and they bow [in worship]."[47]

Uṣūl al-Kāfī, the famous book of Shī'ah narrations, gives the following interpretation of this verse:

"One day, *Ameer al-Mu'mineen* [the Commander of the Believers, i.e., 'Alī] was offering his noon prayer and had completed the first two *rak'ahs.* He was wearing a costly

---

[47] *Sūrah al-Mā'idah,* 5:55.

mantle worth 2,000 *dirhams.* The Ethiopian emperor had earlier sent it to the Prophet (ﷺ), but he had given it to ‘Alī. At that moment a beggar arrived and cried out, 'O Trustee of Allāh and Commander of the Believers, give some charity to the beggar.' ‘Alī threw away his mantle and indicated with his finger that the beggar should take it. Allāh then revealed this verse [indicating that ‘Alī is the patron or master of the believers]."[48]

Another contemporary Shī‘ah book, *Imāmate* by S. Rizvi, reports the incident in an entirely different manner:

> "One day, a beggar came to the mosque where the Prophet (ﷺ) with his companions were offering prayer. He begged for alms, but nobody gave him anything. The beggar then raised his finger towards the sky and cried out, 'O Allāh, be a witness that I came to the Prophet's mosque and nobody gave me a thing.' ‘Alī at that time was bowing in *rukū‘*. He pointed his little finger on which was a ring towards the beggar, who then came forward and took it from ‘Alī's hand. Allāh then revealed this verse declaring ‘Alī to be the master of the believers."[49]

The following are refutations of the Shī‘ah contentions:

a) All the pronouns in this verse are plural. If Allāh had meant ‘Alī alone, the Qur’ān would have used the singular form.
b) It is universally known that ‘Alī was a very poor man who

---

[48] *Uṣūl al-Kāfī,* p. 177.
[49] *Imāmate,* p. 36.

would not be likely to have worn a 2,000 *dirham* cloak. Shī'ah sources also testify to this effect. For example: "When the Prophet (ﷺ) arranged Fāṭimah's marriage to 'Alī, Fāṭimah said to the Prophet (ﷺ), 'The ladies of Quraysh taunt me that your father has given you in marriage to a person who is destitute.'"[50]

c) The beggar who came to the Prophet's mosque addressed 'Alī as the trustee of Allāh and commander of the believers, showing that the beggar was a Muslim. Thus, he could not have expected that people would respond to him during the prayer and would have waited until its completion.

d) One should note that according to the narration, the Prophet (ﷺ) ignored the beggar and continued his prayer. All those present followed the Prophet (ﷺ), but 'Alī acted independently. By responding to the beggar during prayer, he did what was preferred by Allāh according to this interpretation. The implication is that 'Alī excelled the Prophet (ﷺ) in judgement and virtue. Obviously, this is just another of the Shī'ah extrapolations which is far from the truth.

e) The Shī'ah interpretation of the incident also raises questions about 'Alī's devotion and concentration during prayer. Other accounts confirm that even severe physical pain did not distract him from his prayer. Even if the beggar had indeed sought to interrupt him, 'Alī could not have conceded to this breach of Islāmic behavior.

Ibn Katheer, the renowned Qur'ānic commentator, wrote: "Some people, imagining that the last part of the verse refers to one's state while giving *zakāh,* translated it as, 'give *zakāh* while they are bowing [in *rukū'*].' This is absurd. If that contention is accepted, it would mean that paying *zakāh* is

---

[50] *Jalāl al-'Ayūn,* vol. 2, pp. 65 and 179.

most recommended in the position of *rukū'*, yet no scholar ever advocated this. Those who narrated that 'Alī was bowing in *rukū'* when a beggar asked for charity and 'Alī gave him his ring – not one person in the chain of narrators is reliable and trustworthy."[51]

3. Ḥadīth Ghadeer Khumm

Ḥadīth Ghadeer Khumm is the most widely quoted *ḥadīth* by Shī'ahs in support of 'Alī's claim to imamate. Here is its text as quoted from a Shī'ah source:

> "According to a *mutawātir ḥadīth*,[52] when the verse, 'O Messenger, proclaim what has been revealed to you'[53] was sent down, he (ﷺ) addressed a congregation of people at Ghadeer Khumm, saying, 'O people, am I not preferred to all of you?' They said, 'Yes, certainly you are.' He then said, 'To whomever I am *mawlā* [patron], 'Alī too is his *mawlā*.' He then prayed, 'O Allāh, befriend whoever befriends 'Alī and be the enemy of whoever bears his enmity and help whoever helps him and disgrace whoever causes him indignity.' 'Umar then said to 'Alī, 'Congratulations! You are my *mawlā* and the *mawlā* of all believing men and women.'"[54]

Shī'ahs claim that the word "*mawlā*" here signifies "*walī*" and that the Prophet (ﷺ) had nominated 'Alī to be his *walī* (trustee), giving him the right to be his successor and *imām* after him.

---

51 *Tafseer Ibn Katheer,* vol. 1.

52 A *ḥadīth* reported by a large number of narrators through several chains.

53 *Sūrah al-Mā'idah,* 5:67.

54 *Minhāj al-Kirāmah,* p. 94.

Shī'ahs claim this *ḥadīth* to be *mutawātir,* that is, narrated by so many different chains that its authenticity cannot be doubted. It may be pointed out, however, that this *ḥadīth* is not reported in the authentic sources of *ḥadīth* of al-Bukhārī, Muslim, Abū Dāwūd or an-Nasā'ī. Only Ibn Mājah and at-Tirmidhī have reported it, and at-Tirmidhī has classified it as a weak *ḥadīth.*

An objective study of older Shī'ah sources reveals that the earlier Shī'ah scholars did not use this *ḥadīth* as a mandate for 'Alī's claim of imamate. The following citations clearly prove this point:

a) During his very last sermon the Prophet (ﷺ) said: "Whoever assumes leadership after me – it is incumbent upon him to be kind to those Anṣār (Madinites) who are virtuous and to forgive those Anṣār who may not be virtuous." That was the last time the Prophet (ﷺ) came out of his home and spoke to the people from the pulpit.[55]

   It is evident from this Shī'ah *ḥadīth* that the Prophet (ﷺ) did not specify his successor. Had he nominated 'Alī to be his successor, there would have been a general announcement and instruction to the public.

b) Another narration from a Shī'ah source reads as follows: 'Āmir bin aṭ-Ṭufayl and Zayd bin Qays went to the Prophet (ﷺ) with the intent to kill him. When the Prophet (ﷺ) entered the mosque, 'Āmir asked him, "What shall be my reward if I choose to be a Muslim?" The Prophet (ﷺ) replied, "The same that will be the reward of other Muslims." 'Āmir then said, "I would like you to make me your successor." The Prophet (ﷺ) answered, "Only Allāh has that right."[56] According to another Shī'ah *ḥadīth,*[57] the Prophet (ﷺ) had nominated 'Alī to be

---

[55] *Jalāl al-'Ayūn,* vol. 1, p. 64.

[56] *Ḥayāt al-Qulūb,* vol. 2, p. 223.

[57] *Da'wat al-'Asheerah,* discussed in detail on pp. 28-32.

his successor and heir at the very beginning of his Prophetic mission in Makkah. This declaration was then repeated at the assembly of Ghadeer Khumm before a crowd of several thousand. If these stories were true, the Prophet (ﷺ) would have boldly answered ʻĀmir that Allāh had already nominated ʻAlī to be his successor.

A third narration from an early Shīʻah source reads as follows: "One night [after the election of Abū Bakr to the caliphate] when it became dark, ʻAlī took al-Ḥasan and al-Ḥusayn with him and went from door to door among the houses of the residents and emigrants [in Madīnah] but none except four (and according to another narration only three) agreed to his claim for the caliphate."[58] At that time about 10,000 companions of the Prophet (ﷺ) lived in Madīnah. If only one percent of these noble companions had understood the word "*mawlā*" as the Shīʻahs explain it today, at least 100 of them, whose mother tongue was Arabic, should have agreed with ʻAlī's claim for the caliphate. The fact is, however, that the Prophet's companions did not take the word "*mawlā*" as a mandate for ʻAlī's caliphate.

c) Below is the version of "*ḥadīth* Ghadeer Khumm" as reported in *Sunan at-Tirmidhī*:

"The Prophet (ﷺ) dispatched a military expedition under the command of ʻAlī. With the war booty came a slave girl, whom ʻAlī kept for himself. A few of his companions did not like this, and four of them decided to bring it to the attention of the Prophet (ﷺ). When ʻAlī returned with his unit, one of these persons asked the Prophet (ﷺ) if he knew that ʻAlī had done such a thing. On hearing this the Prophet (ﷺ) turned away his face. The first man was followed by the second one, and

---

[58] *Jalāl al-ʻAyūn*, p. 149.

then the third, but the Prophet (ﷺ) paid no attention to any of them. The fourth man then got up and repeated the complaint. The Prophet (ﷺ) turned toward him with anger showing on his face and said to him, 'What do you want of 'Alī? What do you want of 'Alī? 'Alī is of me and I am of 'Alī. After me, 'Alī is the mawlā of all the believers.' "[59]

It is very clear from this *ḥadīth* that although a few people were unhappy about 'Alī's distribution of the booty, the Prophet (ﷺ) was satisfied with 'Alī's conduct. The word "*mawlā,*" here, expresses the Prophet's trust and confidence in 'Alī and does not relate to his future caliphate. "After me" refers to rank and position, not to time or succession. It was not an occasion for the nomination of his heir but only an assessment of 'Alī's conduct in a particular situation.

It should be added that the descriptions of 'Alī in "*ḥadīth* Ghadeer Khumm" are not limited to him alone. The Prophet (ﷺ) used the same descriptions for other people as well. For example:

The Prophet (ﷺ) said; "Salmān is the mawlā of Madinites."[60]

The Prophet (ﷺ) said to Zayd: "You are our brother and our mawlā."[61]

The Prophet (ﷺ) said: "Al-'Abbās is of me, and I am of him."[62]

The Prophet (ﷺ) said: "He [Julaybeeb] is of me, and I am of him."[63]

---

59 *Sunan at-Tirmidhī,* vol. 2, pp. 212-213.
60 *Mishkāt al-Maṣābīḥ,* p. 293.
61 *Ṣaḥeeḥ al-Bukhārī.*
62 *Mishkāt al-Maṣābīḥ,* p. 570.
63 *Ṣaḥeeḥ Muslim.*

The Prophet (ﷺ) said; "So they [the Ash'arīs][64] are of me, and I am of them."[65]

The author of *Minhāj al-Kirāmah* and a few other Shī'ah scholars also take the word "*mawlā*" in the sense of *awlā,* meaning deserving, preferable or worthier. If this interpretation is accepted, then the word "*awlā*" has been used by the Prophet (ﷺ) for Abū Bakr as well.

'Ā'ishah narrated: "The Prophet (ﷺ) said to me during his terminal illness, 'Send for Abū Bakr and your brother so that I might write something, for I am afraid that someone ambitious might have intentions or someone might say, "I am awlā [more worthy], while Allāh and the believers refuse except Abū Bakr." ' "[66]

After the demise of the Prophet (ﷺ) a number of his companions, on several occasions, differed over the issue of the caliphate. None of the companions or his noble family members ever presented "*ḥadīth* Ghadeer Khumm" in support of 'Alī's right to the caliphate. Is it conceivable that all the companions of the Prophet (ﷺ) including 'Alī himself had forgotten the Ghadeer Khumm incident or had not understood its significance and meaning?

4. Ḥadīth Da'wat al-'Asheerah

This is another often cited Shī'ah *ḥadīth* in support of the claim that the Prophet (ﷺ) nominated 'Alī to be the *imām* and caliph after him:

"It has been narrated by a large number of people that when the verse ﴿وَأَنذِر عَشِيرَتَكَ الأَقرَبِينَ﴾

---

[64]A well-known tribe of Yeman.
[65]*Saheeh Muslim.*
[66]Ibid.

'And warn your closest relatives'[67] was revealed, the Prophet (ﷺ) collected all of Abū Ṭālib's forty children and served them meat, bread and milk. There was one among them who could devour a whole lamb at one sitting and drink a whole ewer full of drink. The entire assemblage had eaten its full, yet it did not appear that they had eaten anything because the food was still there. The Prophet (ﷺ) greeted his guests and then recited the verse [i.e., 26:214] to them and said, 'O sons of 'Abdul-Muṭṭalib, Allāh Almighty has sent me with the truth to all mankind in general and to you in particular. He has commanded me to warn my close relatives against incurring His displeasure. I invite you to two things which are light on the tongue but heavy on the scale which will measure men's deeds [on the Day of Judgement]. With the help of these two things you will become masters of the east and west, and all the nations [of the world] will become your subjects. These two things will also help you to enter Paradise and save you from the Hellfire. They are: you should bear witness that there is no deity except Allāh and Muḥammad (ﷺ) is His messenger. Whoever joins me in this belief and helps me in bringing this message [to success] shall be my brother, my nominated successor, my minister, my heir and the caliph after me.' None of those present gave a reply; thereupon, 'Alī stood up and said, 'I shall help you in this matter.' The Prophet (ﷺ) asked him to be seated and repeated his

---

[67] *Sūrah ash-Shu'arā'*, 26:214.

question, yet everyone kept quiet. ‘Alī again stood up and repeated what he had said earlier. The Prophet (ﷺ) again asked him to sit down. The Prophet (ﷺ) then repeated his words for the third time, yet no one spoke. ‘Alī stood up again and said, 'I shall help you in this task.' At that, the Prophet (ﷺ) said, 'Sit down! You are my brother, my nominated successor, my minister, my heir and my caliph after me.' The assembly then broke up and the people said to Abū Ṭālib, 'Congratulations on his embracing the faith of your nephew, for he has appointed your son a ruler.'"[68]

There is no mention of this narration in any authentic *ḥadīth* literature. In Shī‘ah books it is narrated by Ibn Jareer al-Bughāwī through different chains. One of the persons named in a chain of narrators is ‘Abdul-Ghaffār bin Qāsim Fahd Abū Maryam al-Kareem, whose narrations are rejected by all eminent critics of *ḥadīth.* Ibn Ḥibbān said that ‘Abdul-Ghaffār used to get drunk and lose his senses, while Abū Dāwūd called him a liar. Imām Aḥmad said that he was not reliable and most of the *ḥadīths* narrated by him are false. Ibn al-Madanī said that he used to forge *ḥadīths,* while Imām an-Nasā’ī and Abū Ḥātim considered him worthy of rejection.[69]

Even if this *ḥadīth* is evaluated on the basis of common sense and simple logic, it is hard to accept. During the early days of the Prophet's mission when the verse was revealed, the Muslims in Makkah were so few and weak that they could not even offer prayers openly. No one knew the future of the Prophet's mission, and certainly no one at that time thought his mission would one day lead to the establishment of a state. Thus, there was neither an occasion nor need for the

---

68 *Minhāj al-Kirāmah,* pp. 93-94.
69 *Minhāj as-Sunnah,* vol. 4, p. 81.

nomination of a head of a future state. Furthermore, at that time 'Alī was a mere child, hardly 10 years old, and it is inconceivable that the Prophet (ﷺ) would have nominated a child to be his heir, his minister and his caliph. Had he done so, the Makkan disbelievers would have accused Muḥammad (ﷺ) of seeking to establish a dynasty for himself and his family.

Imām al-Bukhārī relates two different versions of this incident:

> *'Abdullāh bin 'Umar narrated: "When the verse 'And warn your closest relatives' was revealed, the Prophet (ﷺ) invited the Quraysh, and once they had all gathered, he said, 'O sons of Ka'b, save yourselves from the Fire; O Fāṭimah, save yourself from the Fire. It will not be possible for me to save you from the Fire, although I shall continue to maintain relations with you because of our kinship.'"*[70]

> *It is narrated on the authority of Ibn 'Abbās: "When the verse 'And warn your closest relatives' was revealed, the Prophet (ﷺ) ascended to the top of the hill of aṣ-Ṣafā and called out, 'O sons of Fahr! O sons of 'Adī!' In this manner he summoned the various clans of Quraysh until all were there, and those who could not come out had sent their representatives to tell them later what had happened. Abū Lahab was also among those who came. The Prophet (ﷺ) said, 'If I were to say that there is an army preparing to attack you in this valley, would you believe me?' 'Yes,' they cried out, 'We would certainly believe you, for there has never been an occasion when we tested you and did not find*

---

[70] *Ṣaḥeeḥ al-Bukhārī.*

you truthful.' He then said, 'I warn you of a severe punishment from Allāh.' Upon hearing this Abū Lahab said, 'Woe unto you! Was it only for this that you gathered us? May you be ruined all day!' Then Allāh revealed: ﴿تَبَّتْ يَدَا أَبِي لَهَبٍ وَتَبَّ﴾ *'May the hands of Abū Lahab be ruined, and ruined is he.'* "[71]

These authentic *ḥadīths* convey that when the verse was revealed, the Prophet (ﷺ) warned his near relatives on various occasions, but did not mention 'Alī, much less nominate him as his heir and caliph.

5. Ḥadīth al-Qirṭās

According to Shī'ah belief, another weighty argument favor of 'Alī's succession is the important event of the *qirṭās* (a sheet on which to write). What follows is an account from an original Shī'ah source:

> "When during his last illness the condition of the Prophet (ﷺ) grew serious, he said, 'Bring me some ink and paper that I may write an instruction so you will not go astray after me.' Upon [hearing] this 'Umar said that the Prophet (ﷺ) was probably delirious and that the Qur'ān was sufficient for them. Then there arose some sort of argument, so the Prophet (ﷺ) said, 'Go away from me. It is not proper that you quarrel among yourselves in my presence.'"[72]

The Shī'ah contention is that the Prophet (ﷺ) had wanted to dictate a testament in favor of 'Alī. Had he dictated his testament, there would have been no question about the

---

[71] Ibid., vol. 2, p. 702.
[72] *Minhāj al-Kirāmah,* p. 68.

election of a caliph and ‘Alī would have become the caliph as soon as the Prophet (ﷺ) had breathed his last breath. It was ‘Umar who prevented the Prophet (ﷺ) from writing his will and thus deprived ‘Alī of his legitimate right.

The first Sunni objection to this is that Shī‘ahs merely assumed the Prophet (ﷺ) wanted to write a bequest in favor of ‘Alī. Intentions are known only to the person himself and to Almighty Allāh, but the Shī‘ahs claim to know what was in the Prophet's mind at the time of the *qirṭās* incident. In putting the blame on ‘Umar, the Shī‘ahs accord him with the ability to decipher what was in the Prophet's mind at that time.

The *ḥadīth* also raises serious questions regarding the fulfillment of the Prophet's mission. According to other Shī‘ah sources, Allāh had warned the Prophet (ﷺ) that if he did not declare the imamate of ‘Alī, he would have failed to carry out his mission as a prophet, and that it took the declaration of ‘Alī's imamate for Islām to be completed as a religion and accepted by Allāh. If the matter was of such great importance, why did the Prophet (ﷺ) not dictate his will after ‘Umar had departed? According to one narration, the Prophet (ﷺ) lived for three days after this incident and according to another, five days. He could have designated ‘Alī as his successor during that time if he had wished, but he did not do so.

It should be recalled that a basic and generally accepted criterion for the evaluation of *ḥadīth* concerns the chain of narrators. Ibn ‘Abbās, who supposedly narrated this *ḥadīth,* was only thirteen years old at the time the event took place. According to another narration, the *qirṭās* incident happened in a gathering where a number of elder companions of the Prophet and his family members were present. None of them, however, reported this incident.

Sunnis acknowledge this *ḥadīth* since it is also related by al-Bukhārī, but they do not relate it to the nomination of ‘Alī or blame ‘Umar for the incident. They explain it by taking into account other related *ḥadīths,* five of which are presented below:

> *Sa'eed bin Jubayr narrated that Ibn 'Abbās said to him: "It was Thursday, and what a Thursday it was! When the condition of the Prophet (ﷺ) grew serious, he said, 'Bring me something that I might write a document after which you will never err.' Then some people started arguing, although argument should not take place in the presence of a prophet. A few said they were afraid he was talking in a state of delirium while others wanted to ask him. He then said, 'Leave me to myself, for I am in a better state than that to which you invite me.' Then he gave them three instructions: first, to expel all the idolaters from the Arabian peninsula; second, to receive the delegations [from outside Madīnah] as he used to receive them." [Sa'eed bin Jubayr continued], "As for the third, he did not mention it, or he said, 'I forgot it.'"*[73]

> *'Abdullāh bin 'Abbās said: "When the Prophet (ﷺ) was near death, a number of people were present in the room. The Prophet (ﷺ) asked them to bring him something to write on, for he wanted to write something that would save them from going astray. Some of them said that perhaps he was overcome by pain and that they had the Qur'ān, saying, 'Sufficient for us is the Book of Allāh.' When the differences continued and the dispute increased, the Prophet (ﷺ) said, 'Get up [and go].'"*[74]

---

[73] *Ṣaḥeeḥ al-Bukhārī.*
[74] Ibid.

"It was narrated by 'Alī that the Prophet (ﷺ) asked him to bring a tablet to write down something which would prevent them from going astray. 'Alī said that he expected the Prophet (ﷺ) might forget what he wanted him to write, so he asked the Prophet (ﷺ) to tell it to him so that he would commit it to his memory... The Prophet (ﷺ) told him to be careful about prayer, zakāh and the slaves."[75]

'Ā'ishah narrated that the Prophet (ﷺ) said to her during his final illness: "Send for Abū Bakr, so that I might write something, for I am afraid that someone ambitious might have intentions or someone might say, 'I am awlā [more worthy] than Abū Bakr, while Allāh and the believers refuse except Abū Bakr.'"[76]

'Abdullāh bin 'Abbās said: "One day during the Prophet's last illness when 'Alī had left the bedside of the Prophet (ﷺ), people asked him, 'O Abul-Ḥasan, how is the Prophet (ﷺ)?' He replied, 'Praise be to Allāh, he is better today.' Upon hearing this al-'Abbās bin 'Abdul-Muṭṭalib took 'Alī's hand and said, 'By Allāh, after three days you will be ruled by another. By Allāh, I see that the Messenger of Allāh (ﷺ) will die of this illness, for I know how the faces of Banī 'Abdul-Muṭṭalib appear at death. Let us go and ask him about this matter [i.e., the caliphate]. If it is for us, we will know it, and if it is for someone else, we will know it; and he (ﷺ) will speak on our behalf.' 'Alī replied, 'By Allāh, if

---

75 *Al-Musnad.*
76 *Ṣaḥeeḥ Muslim.*

we should ask the Messenger (ﷺ) concerning this matter and he refused it to us, the people will never give it to us after him. By Allāh, I will never ask it of him.'"[77]

One might wonder: if the Prophet (ﷺ) had nominated 'Alī and his successor before a crowd of several thousand on the occasion of Ghadeer Khumm, why would al-'Abbās have advised 'Alī to put this matter before the Prophet (ﷺ) again? Moreover, if they both knew that the bequest which 'Umar excused the Prophet (ﷺ) from committing to writing was in favor of 'Alī and the opportunity for writing it had offered itself again, why did 'Alī refrain from taking advantage of it? Shī'ah scholars have not yet answered these pertinent questions.

In summary, none of the above-mentioned *ḥadīths* connect this incident to 'Umar, nor do they show that the Prophet (ﷺ) intended to nominate 'Alī as his caliph or *imām*. On the contrary, one of them reveals that he favored Abū Bakr, while another shows that 'Alī deliberately avoided asking the Prophet (ﷺ) anything concerning the future leadership of the *ummah*.

The Shī'ahs have always been selective in quoting and interpreting *ḥadīths* and other events of history. They quote only those that corroborate their beliefs and completely ignore others. Shī'ah scholars not only practice selective perception but also ignore the science of *ḥadīth* criticism by which the acceptability of a narration is determined. Their only concern is to uphold their own point of view.

6. Ḥadīth ath-Thaqalayn

Yet another *ḥadīth* quoted by Shī'ah scholars in support of 'Alī's right to imamate is as follows:

> It was narrated by a great number of people that the Prophet (ﷺ) said: "I am leaving with you

---

[77] *Ṣaḥeeḥ al-Bukhārī.*

> two weighty things [*thaqalayn*]; as long as you hold on to them, you will not go astray. They are the divine Book and my family members [*ahl al-bayt*]. These twins shall not separate until they come to me at the spring [of al-Kawthar on the Day of Judgement]."[78]

Here again, Shī'ah scholars have followed the pattern of quoting what complies with their beliefs and ignoring authentic *ḥadīths* which refute their point of view, such as the following:

> *The Prophet (ﷺ) said: "I am leaving with you two things after which you will not go astray: the Book of Allāh and my sunnah. They will not separate until they come to me at the spring [of al-Kawthar]."*[79]

> *"Someone said to the Prophet (ﷺ) after hearing one of his sermons, 'O Messenger of Allāh, this appears to be a farewell address, so what will be your last message to us?' The Prophet (ﷺ) said, 'My last message to you is to fear Allāh. Listen to and obey your leader, even if he is an Abyssinian slave. He who lives after me will witness many differences, so adhere to my sunnah and the sunnah of the rightly guided caliphs. Hold tight to it and beware of innovations, for every innovation is error.'"*[80]

> *Zayd bin Arqam reported: "The Prophet (ﷺ) addressed us near the well of Khumm between Makkah and Madīnah. After uttering praises to Allāh, he said, 'O People, I am but a human*

---

[78] *Minhāj al-Kirāmah,* p. 98.
[79] Al-Ḥākim – *ṣaḥeeḥ.*
[80] Abū Dāwūd, at-Tirmidhī and Ibn Mājah – *ṣaḥeeḥ.*

being to whom the messenger of my Lord [i.e., the angel of death] is about to come, and I must respond. I am leaving two weighty things with you. One of these is the Book of Allāh, so adhere to it and seek guidance from it.' He then exhorted them to follow the Qur'ān. Then he added, 'And my ahl al-bayt [family members]. I remind you of [your duty to] my family members.' The narrator [Zayd] was then asked, 'Who are his family members? Are not his wives from his family members?' [Zayd] replied, 'His wives are from his family members, but [also] they are those forbidden to accept zakāh after him: the families of 'Alī, 'Aqeel, Ja'far and al-'Abbās.'"[81]

One can derive the following conclusions from the above *ḥadīths*: The Prophet (ﷺ) advised the *ummah* to follow the teachings of the Qur'ān and act upon the guidance provided by it. The Qur'ān was to be accorded the first preference, followed by the *sunnah* of the Prophet (ﷺ). These were specified as the two basic sources of guidance. The *sunnah* of the rightly guided caliphs was included with the Prophet's *sunnah*. None of the above-mentioned *ḥadīths* suggest directly or indirectly that the imamate or caliphate after the Prophet's death should be vested or confined to his family members.

7. Ḥadīth of Noah's Ark

Here is another *ḥadīth* cited by Shī'ahs in support of 'Alī's right the to imamate:

> The Prophet (ﷺ) said: "The example of my family (*ahl al-bayt*) is like that of Noah's ark;

---

[81] *Ṣaḥeeḥ Muslim.*

whoever is with it is saved, and whoever remains behind is drowned."[82]

Shī'ahs interpret this *ḥadīth* to mean that after the Prophet (ﷺ), it is *ahl al-bayt* who was to steer the ship of the Muslim *ummah.* 'Alī, being closest to the Prophet (ﷺ), was supposed to be the captain of the ship. Those who refuse his imamate will be doomed like those who refused to board the ark with Prophet Noah. The author of *Minhāj al-Kirāmah* said, "This *ḥadīth* proves that it is incumbent upon all Muslims to lend their support to *ahl al-bayt,* and since 'Alī is the chief among *ahl al-bayt,* obedience to him is a duty binding upon all Muslims. He alone is the *imām,* and only he (and no other companion) has the right to the caliphate."[83]

This *ḥadīth* is not present in any of the books of authentic *ḥadīths.* Imām Ibn Taymiyyah, the famous scholar of the eighth century, rejected this *ḥadīth* on the basis that none of the narrators are known as trustworthy.[84]

8. Ḥadīth al-Ḥaqq

Shī'ahs use the upcoming narration as an argument that the right to the caliphate was 'Alī's alone and that the caliphate of the three who preceded him was illegal:

> The Prophet (ﷺ) said: "The *ḥaqq* [i.e., right or truth] is with 'Alī, and 'Alī is on the side of the truth; it goes which ever way he goes."[85]

From this the Shī'ahs argue that 'Alī is the criterion of truth, and hence, the legitimate *imām* and caliph of the Muslim *ummah.* This *ḥadīth* is part of one of 'Alī's sermons in which

---

[82] *Minhāj al-Kirāmah,* p. 98. The *ḥadīth* was narrated by al-Bazzār and has been graded as dha'eef (weak).

[83] Ibid., p. 28.

[84] *Minhāj as-Sunnah,* vol. 4, p. 105.

[85] *Minhāj al-Kirāmah,* pp. 54-55.

he enumerates his own merits. The whole sermon is so full of praise for himself that Sunnis find it difficult to believe that a man of ʻAlī's humility and piety could indulge in such self-acclaim. Moreover, no book of *ḥadīth* or history has recorded this saying. *Nahjul-Balghah,* which is supposed to be the most comprehensive collection of ʻAlī's sermons and letters, does not even mention it.

There is, however, a *ḥadīth* recorded in *Sunan Abī Dāwūd* which says that while praying for ʻAlī, the Prophet (ﷺ) said:

> *"May Allāh have mercy upon ʻAlī. O Allāh, make truth the companion of ʻAlī so he will go whichever way it goes."*

According to this *ḥadīth,* the Prophet (ﷺ) supplicated that truth would always be with ʻAlī, and Sunnis are certain that ʻAlī always adhered to the truth. Thus they recognize, respect and love ʻAlī as one of the four rightly guided caliphs but also believe that the criterion for truth is none other than the Prophet (ﷺ) himself.

9. Ḥadīth al-Manzilah

In *Ṣaḥeeḥ al-Bukhārī* and *Ṣaḥeeḥ Muslim* there is a narration by Saʻd bin Abī Waqqāṣ stating:

> *"When the Prophet (ﷺ) was leaving for the Tabūk expedition, he left ʻAlī in charge of his household in Madīnah. ʻAlī said, 'Are you leaving me among the children and women?' The Prophet (ﷺ) replied, 'Would you not accept to be in the same position to me as Aaron was to Moses, except that there will be no prophet after me?' "*

In Shīʻah books this is called *ḥadīth al-manzilah,* which means "position." The interpretation of Shīʻahs is that the Prophet (ﷺ) appointed ʻAlī to be his minister. Thus, ʻAlī is his legitimate successor.

Sunnis point out that Aaron was the elder brother of Moses and did not succeed him as caliph or *imām.* 'Alī's likeness to Aaron was in his close relationship and having been considered as a minister or assistant.

Then there is the additional fact that when the Prophet (ﷺ) left Madīnah for the Tabūk expedition he had 30,000 companions with him (the largest army that took part in an expedition during the Prophet's lifetime, and it was his last). Although the Prophet (ﷺ) personally lead the expedition, he entrusted command of the army to Abū Bakr. According to another *ḥadīth,* he (ﷺ) appointed Ibn Umm Maktūm to act as his deputy in Madīnah and 'Alī was charged with only the responsibility of his family members. Therefore, Sunnis do not take this incident as a mandate for 'Alī's imamate after the Prophet (ﷺ).

In conclusion, objective study of each of the arguments presented by Shī'ahs in the preceding pages reveals two things. Firstly, the Shī'ahs are very selective, quoting only those narrations that corroborate their beliefs and ignoring authentic *ḥadīths* related to the subject in question. Secondly, Shī'ahs give their own interpretations of their narrations, generally disregarding the accepted guidelines for the study and interpretation of *ḥadīth.* The same holds true with respect to Shī'ah quotations from the Qur'ān. They either quote a verse out of context or quote only a portion of the verse.

In addition, the Qur'ānic interpretations of the Shī'ahs are always associated with an incident, where the event and not the verses serve as the basis of their arguments. Thus, the Shī'ah belief in the imamate of 'Alī is based on the incident of Ghadeer Khumm. Similarly, the Shī'ah belief in the infallibility of the *imāms* is based on the *kisā'* incident. The Shī'ahs quote verse 33:33 in support of 'Alī's right to the imamate but base their interpretations on the beggar incident which they associate with the verse. Without their interpretations of the alleged incidents, none of these verses lend the least support to the Shī'ah position. The fact remains that the Qur'ān does not contain a single explicit verse that calls for belief in imamate, and there is not a single authentic *ḥadīth* wherein the Prophet (ﷺ) nominated 'Alī to succeed him as *imām* or caliph.

10. The Superiority of 'Alī

Among the Shī'ah arguments for imamate is that 'Alī surpasses the entire Muslim *ummah* in excellence and is therefore the most worthy successor to the Prophet (ﷺ). They offer the following in support of Shī'ah belief:

- The narrator said that he heard 'Alī say: "We are Allāh's eyes, His hands, His sides and His gateway."[86]
- Imām al-Bāqir said: "'Alī was *muḥaddath,* that is, the angels used to talk to him."[87]
- 'Alī said: "I am the one in whose command Allāh has put the clouds, lightening, thunder, darkness, rivers, mountains, stars, moon and the sun. I am the leader and the guide of this *ummah.*"[88]
- The Prophet (ﷺ) said to 'Alī: "You possess a number of attributes which even I do not have: You have a wife who is Fāṭimah, and I do not have one like her. You have a progeny of sons, whereas I do not have sons. Your mother-in-law is none but Khadījah, whereas I do not have one like her. A [noble] man, Ja'far, is your brother, whereas I do not have a brother."[89]
- It is narrated by more than one authority that the Prophet (ﷺ) said: "Allāh Almighty has granted superiority to my brother, 'Alī, in so many respects that they are beyond reckoning. Whoever acknowledges them and speaks of them – Allāh will forgive all his sins, both past and future.

---

86 *Uṣūl al-Kāfī,* p. 309.

87 Ibid., p. 308.

88 *Ḥayāt al-Qulūb,* p. 436.

89 *Biḥār al-Anwār,* vol. 5, p. 511.

Whoever hears them spoken will be pardoned for all his sins of hearing, and whoever sees them written will be pardoned for all his sins of sight. To cast a glance at 'Alī's face is an act of worship and to talk about him is also an act of worship. Allāh Almighty will not accept the faith of those who refuse to believe in his *wilāyah* [succession] or of those who do not bear enmity for his enemies."[90]

- Ibn 'Abbās narrated that the Prophet (ﷺ) said: "If all the trees in the world were made into pens and all the oceans converted into ink and all the *jinn* were made to count and all the humans were to write, it would not be possible to enumerate all the points which make for the superiority of 'Alī."[91]

Sunnis raise the following objections: First, what is stated in these narrations is contrary to the basic teachings of the Qur'ān and *sunnah,* such as the attribution of characteristics to a human being which can belong only to Allāh. Second, these accounts are not present in any of the authentic sources of *ḥadīths.* Third, the claims attributed to 'Alī are contrary to the humility and piety for which he is well known. It is obvious that these are nothing but fabricated Shī'ah stories.

Sunnis consider all of the aforementioned a discredit to the Prophet's mission. The Qur'ān states that Muḥammad (ﷺ) was sent to improve the condition of mankind and purify the believers through his teachings:

﴿لَقَدْ مَنَّ اللهُ عَلَى الْمُؤْمِنِينَ إِذْ بَعَثَ فِيهِمْ رَسُولاً مِنْ أَنفُسِهِمْ يَتْلُوا عَلَيْهِمْ آيَاتِهِ وَيُزَكِّيهِمْ وَيُعَلِّمُهُمُ الْكِتَابَ وَالْحِكْمَةَ وَإِنْ كَانُوا مِنْ قَبْلُ لَفِي ضَلَالٍ مُبِينٍ﴾

---

90 *Minhāj al-Kirāmah,* pp. 51-52.

91 Ibid., p. 52. Compare this statement with verses 18:109 and 31:27 of the Qur'ān which describe Allāh's endless knowledge.

"Certainly did Allāh confer favor upon the believers when He sent among them a Messenger from themselves, reciting to them His verses and purifying them and teaching them the Book [i.e., the Qur'ān] and wisdom,[92] *although they had been before in manifest error."*[93]

If one believes that the Prophet (ﷺ) repeatedly gave testament in favor of 'Alī's imamate and yet his companions and closest associates gave allegiance instead to Abū Bakr, this would imply that the Prophet (ﷺ) had failed in purifying the believers. Similarly, if the thousands of believers in Madīnah at the time of the Prophet's demise had all forgotten his bequest for 'Alī's immediate succession and willingly chose Abū Bakr instead, it would imply that the revolution which the Prophet (ﷺ) brought forth was so short lived that the moment he closed his eyes his companions forgot him and went against his instruction.

In the same way, if one believes that there were more than 10,000 believers from different parts of Arabia present at Ghadeer Khumm where the Prophet (ﷺ) told them that 'Alī was to succeed him and then delegations came from all over Arabia to offer allegiance to Abū Bakr, would it not mean that the authority of the Prophet (ﷺ) was short lived and immediately forgotten?

Although it is true that 'Alī aspired to be caliph, history has not recorded a single instance where he referred his claim to a Qur'ānic verse or *ḥadīth* of the Prophet (ﷺ). Islāmic history also bears witness that he did offer his allegiance to the first three caliphs. The Shī'ahs acknowledge this as well but add that 'Alī's allegiance was based on *taqiyyah* (dissimulation or deception)[94] and that he did not believe in the legitimacy of their succession to the caliphate.

---

[92]The Prophet's *sunnah.*

[93]*Sūrah Āli 'Imrān,* 3:164.

[94]See the chapter entitled, "The Doctrine of Taqiyyah," p. 84.

Sunnis reply that if 'Alī's allegiance to the three other caliphs was based on dissimulation, he would have at least spoken the truth once he himself became the caliph and *imām.* But he never questioned their integrity or challenged their legitimacy, not before or during his caliphate. In addition, neither the Prophet (ﷺ) nor any of his companions considered 'Alī superior to the rest of the Muslim *ummah.*

Historical realities coupled with logic further serve to negate the claim that 'Alī had been appointed as leader of the *ummah* during the lifetime of the Prophet (ﷺ). Had it been so, the disbelievers of Makkah, always eager to discredit the Prophet (ﷺ), would have seized the opportunity to publicly charge that he was out to build a kingdom or base of power for himself and his descendants. The same would have been said later by the Jews and hypocrites of Madīnah. Yet, the assertion by the Quraysh that he was a poet, a madman or a magician seemed more credible to them than an accusation that he was seeking to establish a family dynasty simply because there was no evidence to back it up. Similarly, enemies of Islām in every age thereafter would have been only too happy to reduce Muḥammad's mission to a quest for power and dynasty if they could have found the least evidence to support such a theory. The fact that they could not speaks for itself.

Whenever the Prophet (ﷺ) left Madīnah, it was his practice to nominate a deputy and assign to him the administrative responsibilities of the state. The following information relates to these appointments:

Name of Deputy and Number of Times Appointed:

Name	Times	Name	Times
'Uthmān bin 'Affān	2	'Abdullāh bin Rawāḥah	1
Zayd bin al-Ḥārithah	2	Sa'd bin 'Ubādah	1
Abū Salamah bin 'Abdul-Asad	1	Ibn Umm Maktūm	9
Sibaa' bin 'Arfa<u>th</u>ah	3	Sa'd bin Mu'ādh	1
Maḥmūd bin Aslamah al-Anṣārī	3		

It may be noted that the Prophet (ﷺ) did not once appoint 'Alī to be his deputy in Madīnah. If he had intended 'Alī to be his successor, he should have at least symbolically nominated 'Alī to be his deputy on one occasion.

During the expedition of Tabūk in 9 A.H., the Prophet (ﷺ) appointed Abū Bakr as commander of the army. The Prophet (ﷺ) also nominated Abū Bakr to lead the first *ḥajj* caravan from Madīnah and direct the *ḥajj* rituals. During his final illness the Prophet (ﷺ) appointed Abū Bakr to be *imām* (leader) of the congregational prayer. These historical facts are not denied even by the Shī'ahs. Again, there is no indication that 'Alī was being considered by the Prophet (ﷺ) for succession.

The following quotations from the book *Nahjul-Balghah,* described as a collection of 'Alī's speeches, confirm his acceptance of the three who preceded him as caliph:

> After uttering praises to Allāh, 'Alī said: "Verily, Allāh sent Muḥammad (ﷺ) as His Messenger and made him the means for turning people away from the paths of sin and wrongdoing, thereby saving them the punishment of the Hereafter. He also made him the means for bringing peace and harmony [among the believers], whereas before him there was discord and dissension. Allāh then recalled him unto Himself, and the believers made Abū Bakr his caliph. Later, Abū Bakr nominated 'Umar as his successor. Both displayed exemplary conduct and maintained justice and equality. So we found them ruling over the *ummah* before us, although we, being the Prophet's family members, had a greater right to the caliphate. We, [however], forgave them."[95]

[95]Commentary of *Nahj al-Balāghah,* p. 447.

> When 'Alī became caliph, he wrote a letter to the people of Egypt through his governor Qays bin Sa'd. After praising Allāh and His Messenger (ﷺ), he wrote: "When the Prophet's mission was fulfilled, Allāh the Almighty recalled him unto Himself. After him the Muslims successively selected two caliphs, Abū Bakr and 'Umar, who kept to the right path, conducted themselves completely according to the Book [i.e., the Qur'ān] and the *sunnah,* and made no departure from the practice of the Prophet (ﷺ). When they were gone the man who succeeded them as caliph did certain things to which the *ummah* objected, and he was killed. The people then came to me and pledged their allegiance to me [as their elected caliph]."[96]

The above citations from a Shī'ah source clearly negate the concept of 'Alī's claim to succession at the death of Prophet Muḥammad (ﷺ). On the contrary, they give his testimony as to the righteousness of Abū Bakr and 'Umar and the legality of the elected caliphate.

THE CALIPHATE AND THE PROPHET'S COMPANIONS

A belief in the imamate of 'Alī clearly results in the denial of the legitimacy of the caliphate of Abū Bakr, 'Umar and 'Uthmān. Such belief also implies that the Prophet's companions, who pledged their support to these caliphs, betrayed the most sacred trust of the Prophet (ﷺ). Based on this viewpoint, the Shī'ahs despise and degrade most of the Prophet's companions and assert that all of them except three gave up Islām after the Prophet's death. The following quotations serve as examples:

---

[96]Ibid., p. 1116.

> "After the death of the Prophet (ﷺ), all his companions gave up Islām except three. These were Miqdād, Abū Dharr and Salmān."[97]

> The only persons present at the burial of the Messenger of Allāh (ﷺ) were 'Alī, al-'Abbās, the two sons of al-'Abbās, and Usāmah bin Zayd. Abū Bakr, 'Umar and the rest of the companions were gathered in Saqeefah.[98]

> "No companion of the Prophet (ﷺ) ever came to offer condolence to the family members of the Prophet (ﷺ) when he died."[99]

A basic issue thus rests on confirmation of the integrity of the Prophet's companions and the fact that their conduct could not have been contrary to the instruction of Allāh's Messenger (ﷺ).

The issue should first be looked at from a historical perspective. When the initial revelations of the Qur'ān began in Makkah and the Prophet (ﷺ) made his declaration of prophethood, the idol worshippers (who were powerful and influential in Makkan society) became the Prophet's most bitter enemies, subjected him and his companions to the utmost physical and mental torture, attempted to kill him, and finally drove him and his companions out of Makkah. The only group of people who accepted his message, supported his mission, struggled with him for its propagation, and sacrificed their properties and lives to protect him and his message was the believers who were none other than the Prophet's companions. This was the group that witnessed the gradual revelation of the Qur'ān, the evolution of the Prophet's

---

[97] *Furu' al-Kāfī,* vol. 2, p. 115.

[98] See *Islamic Affairs,* vol. 2, 1979. The fact is that this meeting, in which Abū Bakr was elected caliph, took place well before the Prophet's burial. For two days after his death people continued to enter the small room in tens to pray over him.

[99] Ibid.

following from a weak community to a powerful state, and the completion of Islām as a way of life. Thus, whatever the Prophet (ﷺ) said, whatever he did, whatever he accomplished, and above all, whatever was revealed to him as Qur'ān was witnessed, received, memorized and recorded by these people. It was this group who transmitted all this to succeeding generations. Consequently, what exists today of the Qur'ān and *sunnah* and what is known of the Prophet (ﷺ) – his sacred life, his noble mission, his teachings, his government, his habits, his conduct, the success he achieved, etc. – was transmitted through this channel of loyal companions. If the integrity of the Prophet's companions should be in doubt, there would remain no basis on which to accept the Qur'ān or the *sunnah* of the Prophet (ﷺ). It is well known that the initial collection of the Qur'ān's text was done by the Prophet's companions and that the first written copy of the Qur'ān was compiled during the caliphate of Abū Bakr upon the recommendation of 'Umar. This copy was then entrusted to Ḥafṣah, one of the Prophet's wives and daughter of 'Umar. During the entire period of Abū Bakr and 'Umar's caliphate this Qur'ān served as a reference for the entire Muslim *ummah.* It is also universally agreed that the Qur'ān was standardized in the Qurayshī dialect during the caliphate of 'Uthmān and that it represents the consensus of the companions, all of whom agreed that it contained exactly what Muḥammad (ﷺ) had received as revelation from Allāh.

◆ The Shī'ah Position Regarding the Ṣaḥābah

The popular Shī'ah belief regarding the Prophet's companions is as follows:

> "After the death of the Prophet (ﷺ) all of his companions became disbelievers except three. They were Miqdād, Abū Dharr and Salmān."[100]

---

[100] *Furu' al-Kāfī,* vol. 3, p. 115; *Ḥayāt al-Qulūb,* vol. 2, p. 600; *Biḥār al-Anwār,* p. 46.

According to numerous Shī'ah traditions, the first three caliphs not only died as disbelievers but proved to be the greatest enemies of Islām:

> "Al-Mahdī will order Abū Bakr and 'Umar to be tied up against a tree and will then order fire to appear from the ground and burn their bodies. He will then order wind to blow their ashes into rivers. He will kill the two caliphs thus a thousand times from morning until evening. The two will then be brought to life, and Allāh will throw them wherever He pleases."[101]

A respected Shī'ah scholar, al-Majlisī, has added:

> "When Imām al-Mahdī appears he will order that the walls of the Prophet's tomb be broken. He will then order the bodies of Abū Bakr and 'Umar to be removed from their graves, their shrouds removed, and their bodies hung on a dry tree."[102]

> "It is narrated in a number of traditions that 'Alī and all the *imāms* have called Abū Bakr the Pharaoh, 'Umar the Hāmān, and 'Uthmān the Qārūn of this *ummah*."[103]

Ḥafṣah, who was entrusted with the first written copy of the Qur'ān also comes under attack along with the Prophet's beloved wife, 'Ā'ishah:

> "One should detest the four idols, namely, Abū Bakr, 'Umar, 'Uthmān and Mu'āwiyah, and

---

[101] *Ḥaqq al-Yaqeen,* p. 217.
[102] *Ḥayāt al-Qulūb,* vol. 1, p. 216.
[103] Ibid., vol. 4, p. 328.

four women, namely, ‘Ā’ishah, Ḥafṣah, Hind and Umm al-Ḥakam."[104]

According to Shī‘ah beliefs, all those noble companions who preserved the initial revelation of the Qur’ān died as disbelievers. Thus, Shī‘ahs have no basis to believe in the reliability of the Qur’ān, not to speak of prophetic *ḥadīths* or the general history of Islām.

◆ The Prophet's Companions According to the Qur’ān

Sunnis refute the false Shī‘ah allegations by taking evidences directly from the verses of the Qur’ān which explicitly speak of the virtues of the Prophet's companions and their exemplary conduct. Moreover, these verses declare Allāh's eternal pleasure with those companions. It has been stated earlier that the companions gave allegiance to Abū Bakr, ‘Umar and ‘Uthmān as their caliphs, and there is no evidence that they believed in the superiority of ‘Alī or the doctrine of divinely nominated *imāms.* Allāh's declaration in the Qur’ān of His eternal pleasure with them establishes the validity of their allegiance to the first three caliphs.

The Shī‘ahs acknowledge these verses but add that Allāh was pleased with the Prophet's companions only during his lifetime. When they later refused to accept ‘Alī's divine right, they thus became disbelievers. Consequently, they were then deprived of Allāh's pleasure.

The logical reply is that if those companions were going to become disbelievers, Almighty Allāh would have known it and warned His Messenger (ﷺ) of their hypocrisy, just as He did about the evil designs of the disbelievers.[105] Fortunately, the Qur’ān has ample testimonies to their faith, righteousness,

---

[104] *Ḥaqq al-Yaqeen,* p. 685.

[105] On the contrary, it has been narrated by Aḥmad, al-Bukhārī, Muslim, Abū Dāwūd and at-Tirmidhī that the Prophet (ﷺ) said: *"Do not revile my companions..."*

conduct and good works, along with declarations of Allāh's rewards for them in both worlds. The following verse serves as an example:

﴿مُحَمَّدٌ رَسُولُ اللهِ وَالَّذِينَ مَعَهُ أَشِدَّاءُ عَلَى الكُفَّارِ رُحَمَاءُ بَيْنَهُمْ تَرَاهُمْ رُكَّعًا سُجَّدًا يَبْتَغُونَ فَضْلاً مِنَ اللهِ وَرِضْوَانًا سِيمَاهُمْ فِي وُجُوهِهِم مِن أَثَرِ السُّجُودِ ذَٰلِكَ مَثَلُهُمْ فِي التَّوْرَاةِ وَمَثَلُهُمْ فِي الإِنجِيلِ كَزَرْعٍ أَخْرَجَ شَطْأَهُ فَآزَرَهُ فَاسْتَغْلَظَ فَاسْتَوَى عَلَى سُوقِهِ يُعْجِبُ الزُّرَّاعَ لِيَغِيظَ بِهِمُ الكُفَّارَ وَعَدَ اللهُ الَّذِينَ آمَنُوا وَعَمِلُوا الصَّالِحَاتِ مِنْهُم مَغْفِرَةً وَأَجْرًا عَظِيمًا﴾

"Muḥammad is the Messenger of Allāh; and those with him are forceful against the disbelievers, merciful among themselves. You see them bowing and prostrating [in prayer], seeking bounty from Allāh and [His] pleasure. Their mark [i.e., sign] is on their faces [i.e., foreheads] from the trace of prostration. That is their description in the Torah. And their description in the Gospel is as a plant which produces its offshoots and strengthens them so they grow firm and stand upon their stalks, delighting the sowers – so that He [i.e., Allāh] may enrage by them the disbelievers. Allāh has promised those who believe and do righteous deeds among them forgiveness and a great reward."[106]

This verse describes a few of the attributes of those who were with the Messenger of Allāh, the Prophet's noble companions, who accepted his message and stood by him through every difficulty. The Qur'ān describes them as

---

106 *Sūrah al-Fatḥ*, 48:29.

merciful among themselves, negating the popular Shī'ah belief that there was bitter enmity between 'Alī and the Prophet's other companions. The verse also describes their attitude in prayer, testifying to humbleness in their hearts.

Consider for a moment the personalities of the people the Qur'ān describes as "those with him." Abū Bakr was the first among the men to accept Islām. Throughout his life he firmly stood by the Prophet's side and was the only companion who accompanied the Prophet (ﷺ) on his journey of migration to Madīnah. The Prophet (ﷺ) was so close to him that he married his daughter, 'Ā'ishah. 'Umar was the companion through whom the Prophet (ﷺ) prayed that Allāh would strengthen Islām. The Prophet (ﷺ) also strengthened personal ties with him by marrying his daughter, Ḥafṣah. 'Uthmān was the companion who had the unique honor of having taken two of the Prophet's daughters in marriage, one after the other. These three were therefore obviously among the closest of "those with him."

﴿وَاعْتَصِمُوا بِحَبْلِ اللَّهِ جَمِيعًا وَلَا تَفَرَّقُوا وَاذْكُرُوا نِعْمَتَ اللَّهِ عَلَيْكُمْ إِذْ كُنتُمْ أَعْدَاءً فَأَلَّفَ بَيْنَ قُلُوبِكُمْ فَأَصْبَحْتُم بِنِعْمَتِهِ إِخْوَانًا وَكُنتُمْ عَلَىٰ شَفَا حُفْرَةٍ مِّنَ النَّارِ فَأَنقَذَكُم مِّنْهَا كَذَٰلِكَ يُبَيِّنُ اللَّهُ لَكُمْ آيَاتِهِ لَعَلَّكُمْ تَهْتَدُونَ﴾

"And hold firmly to the rope[107] *of Allāh all together and do not become divided. And remember the favor of Allāh upon you – when you were enemies and He brought your hearts together and you became, by His favor, brothers. And you were on the edge of a pit of the Fire, and He saved you from it. Thus does Allāh make clear to you His verses that you may be guided."*[108]

---

107 Referring either to His covenant or the Qur'ān.
108 *Sūrah Āli 'Imrān,* 3:103.

This verse directly addressed the Prophet's companions, reminding them that they were enemies before Islām and that Allāh had saved them from Hellfire. The Shī'ahs insist that all those companions who refused to acknowledge 'Alī's right of imamate became disbelievers or hypocrites, but Allāh is saying that He saved them from the Fire, showing that He regards them as believers.

﴿وَالسَّابِقُونَ الأَوَّلُونَ مِنَ الْمُهَاجِرِينَ وَالأَنصَارِ وَالَّذِينَ اتَّبَعُوهُم بِإِحسَانٍ رَضِيَ اللهُ عَنهُم وَرَضُوا عَنهُ وَأَعَدَّ لَهُم جَنَّاتٍ تَجرِي تَحتَهَا الأَنهَارُ خَالِدِينَ فِيهَا أَبَدًا ذٰلِكَ الفَوزُ العَظِيمُ﴾

"And the first forerunners [in the faith] among the Muhājireen and the Anṣār and those who followed them with good conduct – Allāh is pleased with them and they are pleased with Him, and He has prepared for them gardens beneath which rivers flow, wherein they will abide forever. That is the great attainment."[109]

This verse specifically mentions the Muhājireen, who left their homes and families in Makkah and settled in Madīnah for the cause of Islām, and the Anṣār of Madīnah who aided them. Allāh clearly and explicitly states that He is pleased with them and gives them good tidings of Paradise. Needless to say, the first three rightly guided caliphs were foremost among the Muhājireen (emigrants), and those who elected them as caliphs were foremost among both the emigrants and residents of Madīnah.

﴿لِلفُقَرَاءِ الْمُهَاجِرِينَ الَّذِينَ أُخرِجُوا مِن دِيَارِهِم وَأَموَالِهِم يَبتَغُونَ فَضلاً مِن اللهِ وَرِضوَانًا وَيَنصُرُونَ اللهَ وَرَسُولَهُ أُولٰئِكَ هُمُ الصَّادِقُونَ. وَالَّذِينَ تَبَوَّؤُوا الدَّارَ وَالإِيمَانَ مِن قَبلِهِم يُحِبُّونَ

[109] *Sūrah at-Tawbah,* 9:100.

مَن هَاجَرَ إِلَيهِم وَلاَ يَجِدُونَ فِي صُدُورِهِم حَاجَةً مِمَّا أُوتُوا وَيُؤثِرُونَ عَلَى أَنفُسِهِم وَلَو كَانَ بِهِم خَصَاصَةٌ وَمَن يُوقَ شُحَّ نَفسِهِ فَأُولَـئِكَ هُمُ المُفلِحُونَ. وَالَّذِينَ جَاءُو مِن بَعدِهِم يَقُولُونَ رَبَّنَا اغفِر لَنَا وَلإِخوَانِنَا الَّذِينَ سَبَقُونَا بِالإِيمَانِ وَلاَ تَجعَل فِي قُلُوبِنَا غِلاًّ لِلَّذِينَ آمَنُوا رَبَّنَا إِنَّكَ رَؤُوفٌ رَحِيمٌ﴾

"For the poor emigrants who were expelled from their homes and their properties, seeking bounty from Allāh and [His] approval and supporting Allāh and His Messenger, [there is a share].[110] *Those are the truthful. And [also for] those who were settled in the Home [i.e., al-Madīnah] and [adopted] the faith before them. They love those who emigrated to them and find not any want in their breasts of what they [i.e., the emigrants] were given but give [them] preference over themselves, even though they are in privation. And whoever is protected from the stinginess of his soul – it is those who will be the successful. And [there is a share for] those who came after them, saying, 'Our Lord, forgive us and our brothers who preceded us in faith and put not in our hearts [any] resentment toward those who have believed. Our Lord, indeed You are Kind and Merciful.' "*[111]

﴿أُذِنَ لِلَّذِينَ يُقَاتَلُونَ بِأَنَّهُم ظُلِمُوا وَإِنَّ اللهَ عَلَى نَصرِهِم لَقَدِيرٌ. الَّذِينَ أُخرِجُوا مِن دِيَارِهِم بِغَيرِ حَقٍّ إِلاَّ أَن يَقُولُوا رَبُّنَا اللهُ وَلَولاَ دَفعُ اللهِ النَّاسَ بَعضَهُم بِبَعضٍ لَهُدِّمَت صَوَامِعُ وَبِيَعٌ وَصَلَوَاتٌ

[110]The reference here is to properties abandoned by the enemy and their distribution among the Muslims.

[111]*Sūrah al-Ḥashr,* 59:8-10.

﴿وَمَسَاجِدُ يُذْكَرُ فِيهَا اسمُ اللهِ كَثِيرًا وَلَيَنصُرَنَّ اللهُ مَن يَنصُرُهُ إِنَّ اللهَ لَقَوِيٌّ عَزِيزٌ. الَّذِينَ إِن مَكَّنَّاهُم فِي الأَرضِ أَقَامُوا الصَّلاَةَ وَآتَوُا الزَّكَاةَ وَأَمَرُوا بِالمَعرُوفِ وَنَهَوا عَنِ المُنكَرِ وَللهِ عَاقِبَةُ الأُمُورِ﴾

"Permission [to fight] has been given to those who are being fought,[112] *because they were wronged. And indeed, Allāh is competent to give them victory. [They are] those who have been evicted from their homes without right – only because they say, 'Our Lord is Allāh.' And were it not that Allāh checks the people, some by means of others, there would have been demolished monasteries, churches, synagogues, and mosques in which the name of Allāh is much mentioned [i.e., praised]. And Allāh will surely support those who support Him [i.e., His cause]. Indeed, Allāh is Powerful and Exalted in Might. [And they are] those who, if We give them authority in the land, establish prayer and give zakāh and enjoin what is right and forbid what is wrong. And to Allāh belongs the outcome of [all] matters."*[113]

In these verses Allāh has also testified to the selflessness and sacrifice of the emigrants and residents who aided them.

﴿لَقَد تَابَ اللهُ عَلَى النَّبِيِّ وَالمُهَاجِرِينَ وَالأَنصَارِ الَّذِينَ اتَّبَعُوهُ فِي سَاعَةِ العُسرَةِ مِن بَعدِ مَا كَادَ يَزِيغُ قُلُوبُ فَرِيقٍ مِنهُم ثُمَّ تَابَ عَلَيهِم إِنَّهُ بِهِم رَؤُوفٌ رَحِيمٌ﴾

---

112 Referring here to the Prophet's companions.

113 *Sūrah al-Ḥajj,* 22:39-41.

"Allāh has already forgiven the Prophet and the Muhājireen and the Anṣār who followed him in the hour of difficulty after the hearts of a party of them had almost inclined [to doubt], and then He forgave them. Indeed, He was to them Kind and Merciful."[114]

This verse praises the companions who aided the Prophet (ﷺ) during the Tabūk expedition. When the Prophet (ﷺ) made that appeal for help, 'Umar went to his home and divided the provisions of his entire household into two equal halves and presented one half to the Prophet (ﷺ). 'Uthmān made such an enormous donation that the Prophet (ﷺ) declared that nothing 'Uthmān did after that would harm him.[115] Abū Bakr collected everything he had in his home and presented it to the Prophet (ﷺ). The Prophet (ﷺ) asked him what he had left for his family. Abū Bakr answered, "The love of Allāh and His Messenger (ﷺ)."

The verse also mentions those companions whose hearts had wavered so that for a moment they hesitated to join the Prophet (ﷺ). But they did do so, and Allāh declared that He had forgiven them as well. Allāh Himself has praised these companions and forgiven their human weaknesses, but the Shī'ahs continue to harbor grudges against them and find fault with them.

﴿كُنتُم خَيرَ أُمَّةٍ أُخرِجَت لِلنَّاسِ تَأمُرُونَ بِالمَعرُوفِ وَتَنهَونَ عَنِ المُنكَرِ وَتُؤمِنُونَ بِاللهِ وَلَو آمَنَ أَهلُ الكِتَابِ لَكَانَ خَيرًا لَهُم مِنهُمُ المُؤمِنُونَ وَأَكثَرُهُمُ الفَاسِقُونَ﴾

"You are the best nation produced [as an example] for mankind. You enjoin what is

[114] *Sūrah at-Tawbah,* 9:117.

[115] Aḥmad and at-Tirmidhī – *ḥasan.* The *ṣaḥābah* acknowledged that the army for the Tabūk expedition was equipped by 'Uthmān. It consisted of 30,000 warriors.

right and forbid what is wrong and believe in Allāh. If only the People of the Scripture had believed, it would have been better for them. Among them are believers, but most of them are defiantly disobedient."[116]

There is no doubt that this verse is addressed to those who were present in the time of its revelation, i.e., the Prophet's companions. Even the Shī'ahs agree that this verse refers to the Prophet's companions. According to one of their commentaries:

> "A few [scholars] have written that this verse refers to a particular group of emigrants; others have written that it refers to the companions [in general] and that [the entire] *ummah* is also included in it."[117]

The Prophet's companions were not infallible like the Shī'ah *imāms* are claimed to be, but because Allāh promised to forgive them and is well-pleased with them, Sunnis respect and honor them.

﴿وَعَدَ اللهُ الَّذِينَ آمَنُوا مِنكُم وَعَمِلُوا الصَّالِحَاتِ لَيَستَخلِفَنَّهُم فِي الأَرضِ كَمَا استَخلَفَ الَّذِينَ مِن قَبلِهِم وَلَيُمَكِّنَنَّ لَهُم دِينَهُمُ الَّذِي ارتَضَى لَهُم وَلَيُبَدِّلَنَّهُم مِن بَعدِ خَوفِهِم أَمنًا يَعبُدُونَنِي لَا يُشرِكُونَ بِي شَيئًا وَمَن كَفَرَ بَعدَ ذَٰلِكَ فَأُولَٰئِكَ هُمُ الفَاسِقُونَ﴾

"Allāh has promised those who have believed among you and done righteous deeds that He will surely grant them succession [to authority] upon the earth just as He granted it to those before them and that He will surely establish

---

[116] *Sūrah Āli 'Imrān,* 3:110.
[117] Majma al-Bayan, Tabrasi, Tehran, (1274) p. 200.

for them [therein] their religion which He has preferred for them and that He will surely substitute for them, after their fear, security, [for] they worship Me, not associating anything with Me. But whoever disbelieves[118] *after that – then those are the defiantly disobedient."*[119]

Both Sunni and Shī'ah Qur'ānic commentators agree that these verses were revealed in a period when the Prophet (ﷺ) and his companions lived in a state of constant fear. Allāh promised three things: He would give the believers authority in the land, He would establish their religion, and He would change their state of fear to one of security and peace. Islāmic history bears witness that these promises were fulfilled during the caliphates of Abū Bakr, 'Umar, 'Uthmān and 'Alī. In contrast, none of the eleven Shī'ah *imāms* after 'Alī had authority in the land, Allāh did not establish His religion through them, nor did He change the state of fear to one of security during the period of their imamate. Hence, this verse has no meaning if the legitimacy of the rightly guided caliphs is rejected.

﴿الَّذِينَ آمَنُوا وَهَاجَرُوا وَجَاهَدُوا فِي سَبِيلِ اللهِ بِأَموَالِهِم وَأَنفُسِهِم أَعظَمُ دَرَجَةً عِندَ اللهِ وَأُولَٰئِكَ هُمُ الفَائِزُونَ. يُبَشِّرُهُم رَبُّهُم بِرَحمَةٍ مِنهُ وَرِضوَانٍ وَجَنَّاتٍ لَهُم فِيهَا نَعِيمٌ مُقِيمٌ. خَالِدِينَ فِيهَا أَبَدًا إِنَّ اللهَ عِندَهُ أَجرٌ عَظِيمٌ﴾

"The ones who have believed, emigrated and striven in the cause of Allāh with their wealth and their lives are greater in rank in the sight of Allāh. And it is those who are the attainers [of

---

[118] i.e., denies the favor of Allāh or does not live by His ordinance.
[119] *Sūrah an-Nūr,* 24:55.

success]. Their Lord gives them good tidings of mercy from Him and approval and of gardens for them wherein is enduring pleasure. [They will be] abiding therein forever. Indeed, Allāh has with Him a great reward."[120]

These verses refer to the emigrants in particular and the Prophet's companions in general. Those who reject the legitimacy of the three caliphs and the righteousness of the Prophet's companions must point out another group who could fill the description given by Allāh.

The aforementioned are only a few of the Qur'ānic verses that speak of the virtues of the Prophet's noble companions. It should be recalled that all the verses which Shī'ahs present in support of their beliefs in imamate and the superiority of 'Alī are merely based upon narrations associated with them which have been proven to be weak and often forged. Conversely, the previously cited verses are self-explanatory, and one does not have to depend upon any particular interpretation.

Only two alternatives logically emerge from the preceding discussion: either the Prophet (ﷺ) failed to follow the commandments of Allāh and befriended the hypocrites, or the Prophet (ﷺ) fully understood and obeyed Allāh's commandments and did not befriend hypocrites and disbelievers. Acceptance of the second conclusion can only mean that the rightly guided caliphs and other noble companions were neither hypocrites nor disbelievers since all of them enjoyed the love and trust of the Prophet (ﷺ). Moreover, Allāh alluded to the fate of the hypocrites in the Qur'ān:

﴿لَئِن لَّمْ يَنتَهِ الْمُنَافِقُونَ وَالَّذِينَ فِي قُلُوبِهِم مَّرَضٌ وَالْمُرْجِفُونَ فِي الْمَدِينَةِ لَنُغْرِيَنَّكَ بِهِمْ ثُمَّ لَا يُجَاوِرُونَكَ فِيهَا إِلَّا قَلِيلًا . مَلْعُونِينَ أَيْنَمَا ثُقِفُوا أُخِذُوا وَقُتِّلُوا تَقْتِيلًا﴾

---

[120] *Sūrah at-Tawbah,* 9:20-22.

"If the hypocrites and those in whose hearts is disease and those who spread rumors in al-Madīnah do not cease, We will surely incite you against them; then they will not remain your neighbors therein except for a little, accursed wherever they are found, [being] seized and massacred completely."[121]

Islāmic history shows that the hypocrites were driven out of Madīnah within the Prophet's lifetime. On the other hand, the three rightly guided caliphs not only remained in Madīnah but still have the honor of being the Prophet's neighbors in Madīnah. In fact, Abū Bakr and 'Umar are buried under the same roof as the Prophet (ﷺ). Historians and scholars of *ḥadīth* affirm that there were at least 124,000 believers who had the honor of being the Prophet's companions. Ibn Ḥajr al-'Asqalānī has given the description of 12,679 of them by name. All of them pledged allegiance to Abū Bakr, 'Umar, 'Uthmān and then 'Alī as their elected caliphs. Had they betrayed the bequest and trust of the Prophet (ﷺ), they would have also been driven out of Madīnah in disgrace.

Could one then believe that the moment he died all those companions and trusted friends abandoned his instruction and betrayed his most sacred trust, pledging allegiance to hypocrites and disbelievers? Does it stand to reason that out of the approximately 124,000 companions only three demonstrated their loyalty by supporting 'Alī's right to succession? Such a belief could only lead to the denial of what Allāh Almighty has stated in the Qur'ān and discredit the mission of Allāh's Messenger (ﷺ).

---

121 *Sūrah al-Aḥzāb,* 33:60-61.

Sunnis accept that the complete text of the Holy Qur'ān as well as its order and arrangement is according to the revelation of Allāh. They also affirm that the present arrangement of the Qur'ān's text was dictated by Prophet Muḥammad (ﷺ) according to divine instruction through the angel, Gabriel. There have never existed two opinions on this issue since it was confirmed as fact by the consensus of the Prophet's companions. The authenticity of the Qur'ān has never been questioned by any of the Sunni jurisprudence schools – the Ḥanafī, Shāfi'ī, Mālikī, Ḥanbalī, or others less well known. It is universally conceded among Muslims that no alteration was ever effected in the Qur'ān and that it exists today exactly as it was revealed to Prophet Muḥammad (ﷺ). Several verses of the Qur'ān as well as authentic *ḥadīths* of Prophet Muḥammad (ﷺ) uphold this position very clearly. The following are four verses from the Qur'ān which testify to this fact:

﴿وَإِنَّهُ لَتَنزِيلُ رَبِّ العَالَمِينَ. نَزَلَ بِهِ الرُّوحُ الأَمِينُ. عَلَى قَلبِكَ لِتَكُونَ مِنَ المُنذِرِينَ. بِلِسَانٍ عَرَبِيٍّ مُبِينٍ﴾

"And indeed, it [i.e., the Qur'ān] is the revelation of the Lord of the worlds which the Trustworthy Spirit [i.e., Gabriel] has brought down upon your heart, [O Muḥammad], that you may be of the warners in a clear Arabic language."[122]

﴿إِنَّا نَحنُ نَزَّلنَا الذِّكرَ وَإِنَّا لَهُ لَحَافِظُونَ﴾

"Indeed, it is We [i.e., Allāh] who sent down the message, and indeed, We will be its guardian."[123]

---

[122] *Sūrah ash-Shu'arā'*, 26:192-195.
[123] *Sūrah al-Ḥijr*, 15:9.

﴿إِنَّ عَلَيْنَا جَمْعَهُ وَقُرْآنَهُ﴾

"Indeed, upon Us is its collection and [insurance of] its recitation." [124]

﴿بَلْ هُوَ قُرْآنٌ مَجِيدٌ. فِي لَوْحٍ مَحْفُوظٍ﴾

"But this is an honored Qur'ān [inscribed] in a Preserved Slate." [125]

Based upon these and other verses, belief in the reliability and validity of the Holy Qur'ān has always been an integral part of the Muslim's faith.

On the other hand, Shī'ahs have developed their own views about the Qur'ān, which are contrary to those historically accepted by the rest of the Muslim *ummah.* Numerous narrations of Shī'ah *imāms* and the writings of their scholars, some of which will be presented in the following pages, testify to these beliefs.

But first, it must be pointed out that there is a consensus among scholars of the Muslim *ummah* that the entire Qur'ān was recorded during the lifetime of the Prophet (ﷺ). Whenever a verse was revealed the Prophet (ﷺ) would call one of his scribes and dictate to him the revealed verse. He would then indicate the exact placement of the revealed verse within the Qur'ān. In addition, there were a large number of the Prophet's noble companions who had memorized the whole Qur'ān by heart. Thus, at the time of the Prophet's death, the entire Qur'ān had been preserved, not only in written form, but also in the hearts of many of his companions.

During the caliphate of Abū Bakr a large number of companions who had memorized the whole Qur'ān were killed. 'Umar bin al-Khaṭṭāb immediately suggested to Abū Bakr that the whole of the Qur'ān should be collected and

---

124 *Sūrah al-Qiyāmah,* 75:17.
125 *Sūrah al-Burūj,* 85:21-22.

compiled into one volume. Abū Bakr appointed Zayd bin Thābit for this task. All of the written Qur'ān was collected and reviewed by a number of those who had committed it to memory. Thus, the first Qur'ānic manuscript was produced. It was then entrusted to the Prophet's wife, Ḥafṣah bint 'Umar, and was the only complete and authentic reference for the divine revelation, although some other companions had their own personal copies.

Later, when Islām spread to Syria, Iraq, Egypt and Persia, differences arose over pronunciation, and it was feared that deviation would become apparent. Therefore, the third caliph, 'Uthmān bin 'Affān, appointed a commission of four companions including Zayd to standardize the Qur'ān according to the copy that had been kept with Ḥafṣah, which was in the dialect of the Quraysh. He then had it distributed to various centers of the Muslim world to replace any other copies which might at that time have been in circulation. This became known as *al-Muṣḥaf al-'Uthmānī,* which, by consensus of the Prophet's companions, contained the revelation from Allāh exactly as it had been recited by Prophet Muḥammad (ﷺ). The present Qur'ān is reproduced from that *muṣḥaf,* and no doubt has ever been expressed among followers of the Prophet's *sunnah* about its reliability and authenticity.

The Shī'ahs, however, have sought to raise doubts about the Qur'ān's authenticity. The following quotations illustrate:

> "The traditions of Prophet Muḥammad (ﷺ) pointing to the unreliability of the present Qur'ān are numerous. Sayyid Ni'matullāh Hā'irī has pointed out in some of his writings that these traditions number more than two thousand. A number of scholars such as Shaykh al-Muḥaqqiq Dhimād and 'Allāmah al-Majlisī have also referred to these traditions. Another group states that the traditions of the Messenger of

> Allāh (ﷺ) referring to the present Qur'ān are *mutawātir* [i.e., reported by a large number of transmitters]."[126]

> Jābir said: "I heard Imām al-Bāqir say, 'Anyone who says that he has collected the whole Qur'ān is a great liar.'"[127]

These writings plainly state the Shī'ahs' rejection of the present Qur'ān, an inherent and integral part of Shī'ah belief.

It is well known that when the Qur'ānic revelations began in Makkah, 'Alī was about ten years old, and al-Ḥasan and al-Ḥusayn were not even born. Consequently, those *imāms* had no part in the initial recording and preservation of the Qur'ān. 'Alī was indeed one of the scribes of the later revelations, and his contribution in this respect is acknowledged by all. It is obvious, however, that due to his youth he would have not been entrusted, as such, with the task of recording Makkan verses. The Prophet's elder companions thus were the only group of believers who could have been entrusted with the task of memorizing, writing and preserving the revelations received by Prophet Muḥammad (ﷺ) at that stage.

In verse 75:17, Allāh (*subḥānahu wa ta'ālā*) stated that He Himself would guarantee the preservation of the Qur'ān. Included among the noble companions who initially played a major part in its preservation and who, according to Shī'ah doctrine later turned disbelievers, were three of the righteous caliphs. Muslim scholars all know that the Qur'ān of today was collected, compiled, preserved and propagated by those three caliphs.

Shī'ah hatred for the first three caliphs is so intense that every year during the month of Muḥarram, special religious meetings are held for the purpose of cursing and abusing them.

---

[126] *Faṣl al-Khiṭāb,* p. 227.
[127] *Uṣūl al-Kāfī,* p. 39.

These are known as "*tabarru'*" meetings and are an integral part of Shī'ah practice. Often, such gatherings have led to bitter fighting between Shī'ahs and Muslims who defend the honor of the righteous caliphs.

Among those of the Prophet's companions insulted by the Shī'ahs are the Prophet's wives, whom Allāh, the Almighty, regards as the mother of all believers:

﴿النَّبِيُّ أَوْلَى بِالْمُؤْمِنِينَ مِنْ أَنفُسِهِمْ وَأَزْوَاجُهُ أُمَّهَاتُهُمْ﴾

> *"The Prophet is more worthy of the believers than one of another, and his wives are their mothers."*[128]

Ḥafṣah was one of the pious wives, and it was she who was entrusted with the first completed written manuscript of the Qur'ān. The following quotations indicate Shī'ah feelings about her:

> "One should detest the four idols, namely, Abū Bakr, 'Umar, 'Uthmān and Mu'āwiyah, and four women, namely, 'Ā'ishah, Ḥafṣah, Hind and Umm al-Ḥakam."[129]
>
> 'Ayāshī reported from reliable sources that Imām Ja'far aṣ-Ṣādiq said: "'Ā'ishah and Ḥafṣah killed the Messenger of Allāh (ﷺ) by poisoning."[130]

The sources of the aforementioned narrations, *Ḥayāt al-Qulūb* and *Ḥaqq al-Yaqeen,* are two of the most well-known works of Mullā Bāqir al-Majlisī, the renowned Shī'ah scholar of twelfth century *hijrah.* It should be noted that the respected contemporary Shī'ah scholar, Ayatullāh Khomeini, has frequently quoted him in his writings and has recommended to all Shī'ahs al-Majlisī's books, especially *Ḥaqq al-Yaqeen.*

---

[128] *Sūrah al-Aḥzāb,* 33:6.
[129] *Ḥaqq al-Yaqeen,* p. 685.
[130] *Ḥayāt al-Qulūb,* vol. 2, p. 870.

One could thus deduce that contemporary Shī'ah scholars share al-Majlisī's view that the Mother of Believers, who was entrusted with the very first complete manuscript of the Qur'ān, poisoned Prophet Muḥammad (ﷺ).

The following citations from well-known Shī'ah sources represent the Shī'ah perspective on the Holy Qur'ān. These citations are arranged under four of their basic arguments as given below:

1. **The Qur'ān was not the only revealed book:**[131]

◆ The 70 Yard Long Qur'ān

Imām Ja'far said: "We have with us a book. No one knows what that book is. That book is the [original] Qur'ān which is 70 yards long."[132]

◆ Fāṭimah's Qur'ān

The Imām [Ja'far aṣ-Ṣādiq] said: "We have a book of Fāṭimah, and do you know what this book of Fāṭimah is? It is a Qur'ān which is three times larger than the [present] Qur'ān, and I swear by Allāh that it does not contain a single word from your [present] Qur'ān."[133]

◆ Two More Revealed Books

The narrator told Imām Ja'far aṣ-Ṣādiq that [the sects of] Zaydiyyah and Mu'tazilah have gathered around Muḥammad bin 'Abdullāh [the

---

[131] None of the alleged books mentioned in this section are available for reference, although it is said that there are copies of "Fāṭimah's Qur'ān" kept secretly by certain people. Shī'ahs believe that the complete, unaltered Qur'ān was removed from this world with the disappearance of the twelfth *imām,* who will recite it upon his return to earth.

[132] *Uṣūl al-Kāfī,* p. 41.

[133] Ibid., p. 146.

son of al-Ḥasan bin 'Alī]. Then he asked the *imām* if Muḥammad bin 'Abdullāh had any proof for his claim to be *imām.* The *imām* [Ja'far aṣ-Ṣādiq] said, "By Allāh, we have two books in which are written the names of all the messengers [of Allāh] and all those who would ever rule any part of this world. Muḥammad bin 'Abdullāh's name is in neither of those books."[134]

◆ A Book Written by 'Alī

The narrator said: "I heard Imām Ja'far aṣ-Ṣādiq say, 'We have something as a result of which others need us and we need no one. It is a book. The Prophet (ﷺ) personally supervised its writing, and 'Alī wrote it. It contains [the details of] what is lawful and what is prohibited.'"[135]

◆ The Special Qur'ān of 'Alī

"*Ameer al-Mu'mineen* [i.e., 'Alī] had a special copy of the Qur'ān which he personally compiled after the demise of the Prophet (ﷺ). He presented it to the Prophet's companions, but they rejected it. He therefore hid it [in his house]. This Qur'ān was kept by 'Alī's descendants and inherited from one *imām* to another as part of the office of imamate and prophethood. It is now with Imām al-Mahdī. Allāh will soon resolve this problem. He will bring forth that Qur'ān with his reappearance [in the world] and order the people to recite it.

---

134 Ibid.
135 Ibid.

That Qur'ān is different from the existing Qur'ān in its sequence of verses and chapters and also in the addition and deletion of some words. Since truth was with 'Alī and 'Alī was the truth, it is evident that the existing Qur'ān has been altered in both these respects."[136]

2. Some Qur'ānic verses are lost or missing:

The following two Shī'ah "*ḥadīths*" are sufficient to summarize their views regarding the Qur'ān's authenticity. It should be noted that the source of these narrations is *Uṣūl al-Kāfī,* the most respected source of Shī'ah "*ḥadīths.*" The narrations are attributed to two of their most revered *imāms.*

◆ A Qur'ān with Different Verses

Sālim bin Sālim narrated: "A certain person recited a few verses before Imām Ja'far aṣ-Ṣādiq, and I heard words, none of which are seen in the Qur'ān that we recite. Thereupon the *imām* said, 'Do not recite this Qur'ān now but follow the one that others read. When Imām al-Mahdī will reappear, he will then recite this Qur'ān.'"[137]

◆ The Qur'ān Having Four Portions

"Imām al-Bāqir narrated that the Qur'ān was revealed in four portions: one fourth dealing with attributes of the Prophet's family members, one fourth condemning the enemies of the Prophet's family members, one fourth dealing with similes and metaphors, and one fourth dealing with obligatory duties and prayers."[138]

---

136 *Faṣl al-Khiṭāb,* p. 97.
137 *Uṣūl al-Kāfī,* p. 671.
138 Ibid., p. 669.

3. The sequence of verses has been altered in the Qur'ān:

The following quotation summarizes Shī'ah beliefs regarding alterations in the words and verses of the Qur'ān:

> "These *ḥadīths,* particularly the ones narrated by the Prophet's family members, clearly say that the Qur'ān we have today is not the same as what was revealed to the Prophet (ﷺ). A few of its verses are in clear contradiction to Allāh's original revelations, a few of them have been altered, and a few deleted. Surely and certainly, a number of things have been deleted from the Qur'ān, for example, 'Alī's name has been removed from various places. Moreover, the *ḥadīths* also state that the arrangement of the present Qur'ān is not the one which was approved by Allāh and His Messenger. 'Alī bin Ibrāheem al-Qummī also held similar views."[139]

4. Substantial alterations have been made in the words of the Qur'ān:

Shī'ah commentaries of the Qur'ān and their books of "*ḥadīth*" cite innumerable examples of alleged alterations within the Qur'ān. All of these "alterations" deal exclusively with the attributes of 'Alī and his descendants, whom the Shī'ahs consider their *imāms.* If one were to collect all of these citations, he would end up with an entirely new Qur'ān. The following are sufficient to give a glimpse of Shī'ah claims in this regard.

◆ Alterations in *Sūrah al-Baqarah*

﴿وَإِن كُنتُم فِي رَيبٍ مِمَّا نَزَّلنَا عَلَى عَبدِنَا فَأتُوا بِسُورَةٍ مِن مِثلِهِ

139 *Tafseer aṣ-Ṣāfī,* Introduction.

وَادعُوا شُهَدَاءَكُم مِن دُونِ اللهِ إِن كُنتُم صَادِقِينَ﴾

"And if you are in doubt about what We have sent down upon Our Servant [i.e., Prophet Muḥammad (ﷺ)], then produce a sūrah the like thereof and call upon your witnesses [i.e., supporters] other than Allāh, if you should be truthful." [140]

The commentary given about this verse is that Imām Ja'far aṣ-Ṣādiq said: "Gabriel brought this verse [to Prophet Muḥammad] mentioning 'Alī as follows: 'If you are in doubt as to what We have sent down to Our Servant regarding 'Alī...'"[141]

﴿فَبَدَّلَ الَّذِينَ ظَلَمُوا قَولاً غَيرَ الَّذِي قِيلَ لَهُم فَأَنزَلنَا عَلَى الَّذِينَ ظَلَمُوا رِجزًا مِنَ السَّمَاءِ بِمَا كَانُوا يَفسُقُونَ﴾

"But those who wronged changed [those words] to a statement other than that which had been said to them, so We sent down upon those who wronged a punishment [i.e., plague] from the sky because they were defiantly disobeying." [142]

Imām al-Bāqir said: "Gabriel brought this verse to the Prophet (ﷺ) as follows: 'But those who usurped the rights of the Prophet's family members changed the words that were said to them, so We sent down on those who usurped the rights of the Prophet's family members a punishment from the sky because they were defiantly disobeying.'"[143]

---

140 *Sūrah al-Baqarah,* 2:23.
141 *Uṣūl al-Kāfī.*
142 *Sūrah al-Baqarah,* 2:59.
143 *Uṣūl al-Kāfī.*

◆ Alterations in *Sūrah an-Nisā'*

﴿يَا أَيُّهَا الَّذِينَ أُوتُوا الكِتَابَ آمِنُوا بِمَا نَزَّلنَا مُصَدِّقًا لِمَا مَعَكُم مِن قَبلِ أَن نَطمِسَ وُجُوهًا فَنَرُدَّهَا عَلَى أَدبَارِهَا أَو نَلعَنَهُم كَمَا لَعَنَّا أَصحَابَ السَّبتِ وَكَانَ أَمرُ اللهِ مَفعُولاً﴾

"O you who have been given the Scripture, believe in what We have sent down [to Muḥammad (ﷺ)], confirming that which is with you, before We obliterate faces and turn them toward their backs or curse them as We cursed the Sabbath-breakers. And the decree of Allāh is [always] accomplished."[144]

Shī'ah traditions state that Gabriel brought this verse to the Prophet (ﷺ) as follows: "O people, believe in what We have sent down about 'Alī, confirming what is with you..."[145]

﴿وَلَو أَنَّهُم فَعَلُوا مَا يُوعَظُونَ بِهِ لَكَانَ خَيرًا لَهُم وَأَشَدَّ تَثبِيتًا﴾

"But if they had done what they were instructed, it would have been better for them and a firmer position [for them in faith]."[146]

Imām al-Bāqir said: "This verse was revealed as follows: 'But if they had done what they were [actually] told about 'Alī, it would have been better for them...'"[147]

﴿لَكِنِ اللهُ يَشهَدُ بِمَا أَنزَلَ إِلَيكَ أَنزَلَهُ بِعِلمِهِ وَالمَلَائِكَةُ يَشهَدُونَ وَكَفَى بِاللهِ شَهِيدًا﴾

"But Allāh bears witness to that which He has sent down to you. He has sent it down with His

---

144 *Sūrah an-Nisā'*, 4:47.
145 *Uṣūl al-Kāfī*, p. 515.
146 *Sūrah an-Nisā'*, 4:66.
147 *Uṣūl al-Kāfī*, vol. 1, p. 521.

knowledge, and the angels bear witness [as well]. And sufficient is Allāh as Witness."[148]

In *Tafseer al-Qummī* is a narration attributed to Ja'far aṣ-Ṣādiq that this verse was revealed to the Prophet (ﷺ) as follows: "But Allāh bears witness to that which He has sent down to you concerning 'Alī, He has sent it down with His knowledge..."[149]

﴿إِنَّ الَّذِينَ كَفَرُوا وَظَلَمُوا لَم يَكُنِ اللهُ لِيَغفِرَ لَهُم وَلاَ لِيَهدِيَهُم طَرِيقًا﴾

"Indeed, those who disbelieve and commit injustice – never will Allāh forgive them, nor will He guide them to a path."[150]

Al-Kulaynī related from Imām al-Bāqir: "Gabriel revealed this verse to the Prophet (ﷺ) as follows: 'Those who usurp the rights of Prophet's family – never will Allāh forgive them...'"[151] It is also narrated in *Tafseer al-Qummī* that Abū 'Abdullāh (Imām Ja'far aṣ-Ṣādiq) recited this verse as follows: "Those who disbelieved and usurped the right of the Prophet's family member – never will Allāh forgive them..."[152]

﴿يَا أَيُّهَا النَّاسُ قَد جَاءَكُمُ الرَّسُولُ بِالحَقِّ مِن رَبِّكُم فَآمِنُوا خَيرًا لَكُم وَإِن تَكفُرُوا فَإِنَّ لِلّهِ مَا فِي السَّمَاوَاتِ وَالأَرضِ وَكَانَ اللهُ عَلِيمًا حَكِيمًا﴾

"O mankind, the Messenger has come to you with the truth from your Lord, so believe; it is better for you. But if you disbelieve, then

---

148 *Sūrah an-Nisā'*, 4:166.
149 *Translation and Commentary of Qur'ān*, p. 124.
150 *Sūrah an-Nisā'*, 4:168.
151 *Uṣūl al-Kāfī.*
152 *Translation and Commentary of Qur'ān*, pp. 124-125.

indeed, to Allāh belongs whatever is in the heavens and earth. And Allāh is ever Knowing and Wise."[153]

The translation of the Qur'ān by the learned Shī'ah scholar Maqbūl Aḥmad[154] and the famous scholar al-Majlisī has rendered this verse as follows: "O mankind, the Messenger has come to you with the truth from Allāh regarding the *wilāyah* [succession] of 'Alī..."[155]

◆ Alterations in *Sūrah al-Ḥijr*

﴿قَالَ هٰذَا صِرَاطٌ عَلَيَّ مُسْتَقِيمٌ﴾

"[Allāh] said, 'This is a way to Me [that is] straight.' "[156]

Imām Ja'far aṣ-Ṣādiq said: "This verse was recited as follows: 'This way of 'Alī is straight [to Me].'"[157]

◆ Alterations in *Sūrah an-Naḥl*

﴿وَلَا تَكُونُوا كَالَّتِي نَقَضَتْ غَزْلَهَا مِن بَعْدِ قُوَّةٍ أَنكَاثًا تَتَّخِذُونَ أَيْمَانَكُمْ دَخَلًا بَيْنَكُمْ أَن تَكُونَ أُمَّةٌ هِيَ أَرْبَىٰ مِنْ أُمَّةٍ﴾

"And be not like a woman who untwisted her spun thread after it was strong [by] taking your oaths as [means of] deceit between you so that an ummah [i.e., community] may be more plentiful than another ummah."[158]

According to the Shī'ah tradition, this verse was revealed

---

[153] *Sūrah an-Nisā'*, 4:170.
[154] *Translation and Commentary of Qur'ān.*
[155] *Ḥayāt al-Qulūb,* vol. 3, p. 355.
[156] *Sūrah al-Ḥijr,* 15:41.
[157] *Uṣūl al-Kāfī,* vol. 1, p. 521.
[158] *Sūrah an-Naḥl,* 16:92.

to the Prophet (ﷺ) as follows: "And be not like a woman who untwisted her spun thread after it was strong [by] taking your oaths as [means of] deceit between you lest one *ummah* should be more virtuous than your *imāms.*" The narrator said, "The word in *Sūrah an-Naḥl* is *ummah* [and not *a'immah*], but he [the *imām*] answered, 'No, it is *a'immah.*'"[159]

◆ Alterations in *Sūrah al-Kahf*

﴿وَقُلِ الحَقُّ مِن رَبِّكُم فَمَن شَاءَ فَلْيُؤمِن وَمَن شَاءَ فَلْيَكفُر إِنَّا أَعتَدنَا لِلظَّالِمِينَ نَارًا أَحَاطَ بِهِم سُرَادِقُهَا﴾

"And say, 'The truth is from your Lord, so whoever wills – let him believe; and whoever wills – let him disbelieve.' Indeed, We have prepared for the wrongdoers a fire whose walls surround them."[160]

Abū Ja'far said that Gabriel brought this verse to the Prophet (ﷺ) as follows: "The truth is from your Lord concerning the *wilāyah* [succession] of 'Alī, so whoever wills – let him believe; and whoever wills – let him reject the Prophet's family members. Indeed, We have prepared for the wrongdoers a fire..."[161]

◆ Alterations in *Sūrah Ṭā Hā*

﴿وَلَقَد عَهِدنَا إِلَى آدَمَ مِن قَبلُ فَنَسِيَ وَلَم نَجِد لَهُ عَزمًا﴾

"And We had already taken a covenant from Adam before, but he forgot; and We did not find in him determination."[162]

---

[159] *Uṣūl al-Kāfī,* vol. 1, p. 377. "*A'immah*" is the plural of "*imām.*"
[160] *Sūrah al-Kahf,* 18:29.
[161] *Uṣūl al-Kāfī,* vol. 1, p. 53; *Ḥayāt al-Qulūb,* vol. 3, p. 215.
[162] *Sūrah Ṭā Hā,* 20:115.

Imām Ja'far aṣ-Ṣādiq said: "The 'covenant' was concerning Muḥammad (ﷺ), 'Alī, Fāṭimah, al-Ḥasan and al-Ḥusayn and the *imāms* from among their descendants. Ādam forgot them. By Allāh, this verse was revealed to Muḥammad (ﷺ) as follows: 'We had already taken a covenant from Ādam before concerning Muḥammad, 'Alī, Fāṭimah, al-Ḥasan, al-Ḥusayn and the *imāms* from among [their] descendants, but he forgot.'"[163]

◆ Alterations in *Sūrah al-Aḥzāb*

﴿يُصلِح لَكُم أَعمَالَكُم وَيَغفِر لَكُم ذُنُوبَكُم وَمَن يُطِعِ اللهَ وَرَسُولَهُ فَقَد فَازَ فَوزًا عَظِيمًا﴾

"He [i.e., Allāh] will amend for you your deeds and forgive you your sins. And whoever obeys Allāh and His Messenger has certainly attained a great attainment."[164]

In *Uṣūl al-Kāfī* and *Tafseer al-Qummī* it is narrated from Imām Ja'far aṣ-Ṣādiq that this verse was revealed as follows: "He will amend for you your deeds and forgive your sins. And whoever obeys Allāh and His Messenger regarding the *wilāyah* [succession] of 'Alī and his *imāms* has certainly attained a great attainment."[165]

◆ Alterations in *Sūrah ash-Shūrā*

﴿كَبُرَ عَلَى المُشرِكِينَ مَا تَدعُوهُم إِلَيهِ. اللهُ يَجتَبِي إِلَيهِ مَن يَشَاءُ وَيَهدِي إِلَيهِ مَن يُنِيبُ﴾

"Difficult for the polytheists is that to which you invite them. Allāh chooses for Himself

---

163 *Uṣūl al-Kāfī,* vol. 1, p. 153.
164 *Sūrah al-Aḥzāb,* 33:71.
165 *Translation and Commentary of Qur'ān,* p. 512.

whom He wills and guides to Himself whoever turns back [to Him]."[166]

Imām ar-Ridhā said that Allāh's actual words in the Qur'ān were: "Difficult for those who deny the *wilāyah* of 'Alī is that to which you invite them."[167]

◆ Alterations in *Sūrah al-Aḥqāf*

﴿قُل مَا كُنتُ بِدعًا مِنَ الرُّسُلِ وَمَا أَدرِي مَا يُفعَلُ بِي وَلاَ بِكُم إِن أَتَّبِعُ إِلاَّ مَا يُوحَى إِلَيَّ وَمَا أَنَا إِلاَّ نَذِيرٌ مُبِينٌ﴾

"Say, 'I am not something original among the messengers, nor do I know what will be done with me or with you. I only follow that which is revealed to me, and I am not but a clear warner.'"[168]

According to Shī'ah "*ḥadīths,*" this verse was revealed as follows: "I am not something original among the messengers, nor do I know what will be done with me or with you. I only follow that which is revealed to me regarding 'Alī, and I am not but a clear warner."[169]

◆ Alterations in *Sūrah Muḥammad*

﴿ذٰلِكَ بِأَنَّهُم قَالُوا لِلَّذِينَ كَرِهُوا مَا نَزَّلَ اللهُ سَنُطِيعُكُم فِي بَعضِ الأَمرِ وَاللهُ يَعلَمُ إِسرَارَهُم﴾

"That is because they said to those who disliked what Allāh sent down, 'We will obey you in part of the matter.' And Allāh knows what they conceal."[170]

---

166 *Sūrah ash-Shūrā,* 42:13.
167 *Uṣūl al-Kāfī,* vol. 1, p. 514.
168 *Sūrah al-Aḥqāf,* 46:9.
169 *Translation and Commentary of Qur'ān,* p. 602.
170 *Sūrah Muḥammad,* 47:26.

According to Shī'ah tradition, Gabriel brought this verse to the Prophet (ﷺ) as follows: "That is because they said to those who disliked what Allāh sent down to the Prophet concerning 'Alī, 'We will obey you in part of the matter.' And Allāh knows what they conceal."[171]

◆ Alterations in *Sūrah adh-Dhāriyāt*

﴿إِنَّكُم لَفِي قَولٍ مُختَلِفٍ. يُؤفَكُ عَنهُ مَن أُفِكَ﴾

"Indeed, you [disbelievers] are in discordant speech. Deluded away from it [i.e., the Qur'ān] is he who is deluded."[172]

Imām Muḥammad al-Bāqir said that this verse was revealed to the Prophet (ﷺ) as follows: "Indeed, you are in discordant speech concerning the *wilāyah* [succession] of 'Alī." He added, "He who denies the *wilāyah* of 'Alī is deprived of Paradise."[173]

◆ Alterations in *Sūrah al-Mulk*

﴿قُل هُوَ الرَّحمٰنُ آمَنَّا بِهِ وَعَلَيهِ تَوَكَّلنا فَستَعلَمُونَ مَن هُوَ فِي ضَلالٍ مُبِينٍ﴾

"Say, 'He is the Most Merciful; we have believed in Him, and upon Him we have relied. And you will know who it is that is in manifest error.' "[174]

Imām Ja'far aṣ-Ṣādiq said in explanation of this verse: "The Prophet (ﷺ) said, 'And you will know who it is that is in manifest error, O disbelievers! I had informed you of the

---

171 *Uṣūl al-Kāfī,* vol. 1, p. 516.
172 *Sūrah adh-Dhāriyāt,* 51:8-9.
173 *Uṣūl al-Kāfī,* vol. 1, p. 518.
174 *Sūrah al-Mulk,* 67:29.

wilāyah of 'Alī after me. Now, who is in clear error?' This explanation was revealed with the verse."[175]

◆ Alterations in *Sūrah al-Ma'ārij*

﴿سَأَلَ سَائِلُ بِعَذَابٍ وَاقِعٍ. لِلكَافِرِينَ لَيسَ لَهُ دَافِعٌ. مِنَ ا للهِ ذِي المَعَارِجِ﴾

"A questioner asked about a punishment bound to happen to the disbelievers; of it there is no preventer. [It is] from Allāh, owner of the ways of ascent."[176]

Imām Ja'far aṣ-Ṣādiq said that this verse was revealed to the Prophet (ﷺ) as follows: "A questioner asked about a punishment bound to happen to the disbelievers for denying the *wilāyah* of 'Alī, of which there is no preventer."[177]

◆ Alterations in *Sūrah al-Muzzammil*

﴿وَذَرنِي وَالـمُكَذِّبِينَ أُولِي النَّعمَةِ وَمَهِّلهُم قَلِيلاً﴾

"And leave Me [to deal] with the deniers, those of ease [in life], and allow them respite a little."[178]

Uṣūl al-Kāfī contains a narration by Imām Mūsā al-Kāthim that this verse was revealed to the Prophet (ﷺ) as follows: "And leave me [to deal] with the deniers of your will concerning the *wilāyah* [succession of 'Alī], those of ease, and allow them respite a little."[179]

---

175 *Uṣūl al-Kāfī,* vol. 1, p. 517.
176 *Sūrah al-Ma'ārij,* 70:1-3.
177 *Uṣūl al-Kāfī,* vol. 1, p. 518.
178 *Sūrah al-Muzzammil,* 73:11.
179 *Translation and Commentary of Qur'ān,* p. 688.

◆ *Sūrah al-Wilāyah*

A number of Shī'ah scholars claim that the Qur'ān once contained a chapter entitled, "*al-Wilāyah*" ("Succession"), wherein Almighty Allāh mentioned 'Alī's name and declared his immediate succession and imamate after Prophet Muḥammad (ﷺ). Muḥsin al-Kashmeerī, a Persian scholar, has published this alleged *sūrah* of seven verses in his book *Dabastān-e-Mazāhib.* Several editions have been printed and are available in Iran. 'Allāmah Nūrī at-Tabrisī has also mentioned in his book[180] that the chapter *al-Wilāyah* declaring 'Alī's imamate has been deleted from the existing Qur'ān. Professor Noeldek in his *History of the Qur'ān*[181] has reproduced this chapter (*sūrah*) from the Persian book *Dabastān-e-Mazāhib.* The same is reproduced below.

سورة الولاية سبع آيات

بسم الله الرحمن الرحيم

يا أيها الذين آمنوا آمنوا بالنبي والولي اللذين بعثناهما
يهديانكم إلى صراط مستقيم ۝ نبي وولي بعضهما من بعض
وأنا العليم الخبير ۝ إن الذين يوفون بعهد الله لهم جنات النعيم
۝ والذين إذا تليت عليهم آياتنا كانوا بآياتنا مكذبين ۝
إن لهم في جهنم مقاما عظيما إذا نودي لهم يوم القيامة أين
الظالمون المكذبون للمرسلين ۝ ما خلفهم المرسلين إلا
بالحق وما كان الله ليظهرهم إلى أجل قريب ۝ وسبح بحمد ربك
وعلي من الشاهدين ۝

---

[180] *Faṣl al-Khiṭāb*, p. 22.
[181] Vol. II, p. 102.

Its translation is as follows:

1. O you who have believed, believe in the Prophet and in the *walī* [successor], both of whom We sent to lead you to a straight path.
2. The Prophet and the *walī* – they are of one another, and I am the Knowing, the Aware.
3. Indeed, those who fulfill the covenant of Allāh will have Gardens of Pleasure.
4. And those who, when Our verses are recited to them are, of Our verses, deniers –
5. For them in Hell is a terrible position when they will be called, "Where are the unjust, the deniers of the messengers?"
6. He did not create the messengers except in truth, and Allāh would not manifest them for [only] a short term.
7. And exalt with praise your Lord, and 'Alī is among the witnesses.

Perhaps some readers may consider all these citations old and obsolete. The writer would therefore like to conclude this discussion with a quote from the recent Shī'ah *imām,* Ayatullāh Khomeini, who openly declared and reemphasized the Shī'ah claim that the Qur'ān had been altered by the Prophet's companions.

> "Those [companions of the Prophet] who cared only for material gains and worldly powers, those who had no interest in Islām or the Qur'ān, and those who exploited the Qur'ān for their own crooked plans – for them it was very easy to delete those verses of the Qur'ān [i.e., the ones which declare 'Alī's imamate], to modify the heavenly Scripture, and to hide the [true] Qur'ān from the public eye in such a way that it has become a blot for the entire Muslim *ummah* until the Day of Judgment. The

> Muslims' accusation that Christians and Jews altered their heavenly scriptures is proved against the Prophet's companions as well."[182]

One can justly ask the followers of Imām al-Khomeini, since they claim that the real Qur'ān does not exist in this world, "What, then, is the source of knowledge and guidance for the Shī'ahs?"

The above citations are a few examples of Shī'ah teachings in regard to the Qur'ān. Anyone who is interested in pursuing this matter further may obtain more details from *Faṣl al-Khiṭāb fī Ithbāt Taḥreef Kitāb Rabb al-Arbāb* (*Conclusive Proof of Alteration in the Book of the Lord of Lords*). This is a remarkable work of Mirzā Ḥusayn bin Taqiyy, a Shī'ah scholar. The author has collected hundreds of "*ḥadīths*" from Shī'ah *imāms* and quotations from Shī'ah scholars for the purpose of showing that the existing Qur'ān has undergone innumerable alterations. When the book was first published in Tehran in 1298 A.H., it caused great uproar and agitation in Shī'ah circles. Shī'ah scholars were much perturbed to see so many of their "*ḥadīths*" and quotations openly documented in a book. They realized that their secret doctrines about the Qur'ān were now exposed to the rest of the Muslim *ummah.* A number of Shī'ah scholars then hastened to write explanatory notes on the book. A few others openly protested against its publication. The author, Mirzā Ḥusayn, later responded to all the objections of Shī'ah scholars in another book, entitled *Raddu Ba'dhish-Shubuhāti 'an Faṣl al-Khiṭāb fī Ithbāt Taḥreef Kitāb Rabb al-Arbāb* (*A Refutation of Doubts about Conclusive Proof of Alteration in the Book of the Lord of Lords*). Both these books were so widely acclaimed that when the author died in 1320 A.H., he was given the highest Shī'ah honor and distinction bestowed on anyone: to be buried at 'Alī's mausoleum at Najaf in Iraq.

---

[182] *Kashf al-Asrār,* p. 111.

The Shīʻah commentaries on the Qur'ān and books of "*ḥadīth*" narrations have clearly and repeatedly declared the unauthenticity of the existing Qur'ān, but Shīʻahs still claim to believe in the Qur'ān. It is paradoxical that they derive their faith and beliefs from those same books that deny the authenticity of the Qur'ān. One can only explain the disparity between Shīʻah sayings and Shīʻah writings on the basis of their practice of *taqiyyah* (dissimulation), which encourages Shīʻahs to conceal truth under certain conditions and to declare something they do not believe at all.[183] Thus, it is logical to conclude that what is recorded in Shīʻah books is the true Shīʻah belief, while what Shīʻahs state verbally is only *taqiyyah.*

This perhaps explains the reason why Shīʻahs do not memorize the whole of the Qur'ān. On the contrary, the Sunni Muslim *ummah* has always produced innumerable *ḥuffāth*[184] who memorize the entire Qur'ān from beginning to end with precise *tajweed.*[185] Every year in the month of Ramadhān, these *ḥuffāth* recite the whole Qur'ān aloud during *taraweeḥ* prayers before congregations of worshippers. The Qur'ān consists of a little over 6,000 verses and a total of 244,744 words made up of innumerable letters and diacritical marks. To memorize all these verses with the necessary detail of phonetics and punctuation would not be humanly possible but for the will of Almighty Allāh. Through His special blessing Allāh gives this honor to those who have the proper faith and respect for the Qur'ān, while He deprives those who would cast doubts on its authenticity of that blessing.

---

[183]See the following chapter, entitled "The Doctrine of Taqiyyah."

[184]Plural of *ḥāfith,* i.e., one who has memorized the entire Qur'ān.

[185]Defined in Islāmic terminology as "the recitation of the Qur'ān just as it was revealed to Muḥammad, the Messenger of Allāh," which includes observing correct pronunciation and related rulings for every single letter.

THE DOCTRINE OF TAQIYYAH (DISSIMULATION)

The Shī'ah doctrine of *taqiyyah*[186] is one which separates them from the rest of the Muslim *ummah.* It is the foundation of Shī'ah practices, whereas the rest of the *ummah* rejects it categorically.[187]

Belief in *taqiyyah* means that a Shī'ah may conceal the truth and tell a lie under certain conditions. It permits Shī'ahs to preach and practice something outwardly yet deny and reject the same inwardly. It also encourages them to outwardly befriend a person but hate and despise him at the same time. Throughout Shī'ah history their religion has been based on the doctrine of *taqiyyah.* Most of the Shī'ah beliefs would lose their credibility if *taqiyyah* is not practiced. It is mainly for this reason that Ja'far aṣ-Ṣādiq is quoted as saying:

> "Indeed, nine tenths of the religion is *taqiyyah.*"[188]

Shī'ahs have invented a story about 'Alī to support their belief in *taqiyyah.* They claim that Abū Bakr, 'Umar and 'Uthmān were not legitimate successors and that 'Alī was the only true caliph and *imām* after Prophet Muḥammad (ﷺ). They also claim that the three other caliphs usurped the right of 'Alī by deceit and force. Islāmic history, however, shows that 'Alī offered unconditional allegiance to the first three caliphs. The Shī'ah interpretation of that allegiance serves as

---

[186] Concealing one's actual beliefs by pretending others.

[187] Lest anyone be deluded by the claim that this practice is sanctioned in the Qur'ān, the verse (3:28) has limited the allowance of pretense to a particular and temporary circumstance: fear of harm or death at the hands of a hostile, disbelieving enemy. Even then, as Ibn 'Abbās pointed out, it does not extend beyond the tongue to one's actions. Permissibility having been restricted to the dire necessity of self-preservation, deception is obviously unlawful for any other purpose or at any other time.

[188] *Uṣūl al-Kāfī,* p. 482.

the basis for their belief in *taqiyyah.* They assert that 'Alī was fully aware that he was the only legitimate *imām* after the Prophet (ﷺ) but that he put up an outward show of allegiance to the other three caliphs in order to maintain the unity of the Muslim *ummah.* Had 'Alī claimed his right, they assert, the Muslim *ummah* would have split into two warring factions. 'Alī thus chose to practice *taqiyyah* in offering his allegiance to each of the three caliphs, thus maintaining the unity of the Muslim *ummah.*

However, history also shows that 'Alī, during his own caliphate, fought for his legitimate cause in three major battles. So it stands to reason that if the Prophet (ﷺ) had nominated 'Alī to succeed him after his death, it would have been 'Alī's duty to fight for his right and to fulfill the wish of Allāh's Messenger (ﷺ). Hence, the rest of the Muslim *ummah* believes that 'Alī offered sincere allegiance to the three caliphs. It is unfortunate that Shī'ahs associate 'Alī with hypocrisy only to justify their own practice of *taqiyyah.*

The following pages will present the Shī'ah concept of *taqiyyah,* then an analysis of Shī'ah belief with reference to the Qur'ān and *sunnah,* a discussion of the role of 'Alī, and a discussion of the roles of other Shī'ah *imāms* in negating the Shī'ah concept of *taqiyyah.*

The following quotations are self-explanatory and serve to express the Shī'ah doctrine of *taqiyyah*:

> Imām al-Bāqir said: "*Taqiyyah* is my religion and the religion of my father and forefathers. He who does not practice *taqiyyah* is devoid of faith."[189]

> Imām Ja'far aṣ-Ṣādiq said: "Indeed, nine tenths of religion is *taqiyyah.* He who does not practice *taqiyyah* is devoid of religion.

---

[189] *Uṣūl al-Kāfī,* p. 419.

Taqiyyah is mandatory for everything in life except in the case of drinking alcohol and wiping over socks during ablution."[190]

Imām Ja'far aṣ-Ṣādiq said: "You belong to a religion that whoever conceals it – Allāh will honor him; and whoever exposes it – Allāh will disgrace him."[191]

Readers can compare these narrations with basic teachings of the Qur'ān. Allāh, the Mighty and Majestic, said:

﴿إِنَّ الَّذِينَ يَكْتُمُونَ مَا أَنزَلْنَا مِنَ الْبَيِّنَاتِ وَالْهُدَىٰ مِن بَعْدِ مَا بَيَّنَّاهُ لِلنَّاسِ فِي الْكِتَابِ أُولَٰئِكَ يَلْعَنُهُمُ اللَّهُ وَيَلْعَنُهُمُ اللَّاعِنُونَ﴾

"Indeed, those who conceal what We sent down of clear proofs and guidance after We made it clear for the people in the Book – those are cursed by Allāh and cursed by those who [are entitled to] curse."[192]

Here are more Shī'ah narrations regarding *taqiyyah*:

Imām al-Bāqir said: "*Taqiyyah* can be observed for any genuine need. He who practices it has the freedom to determine whether or not his need is genuine."[193]

"Imām Ja'far aṣ-Ṣādiq said, 'Practicing *taqiyyah* is the religion of Allāh.' The narrator asked, 'Truly? Is it part of Allāh's religion?' The *imām* answered, 'Practicing *taqiyyah* is the

[190] Ibid., p. 482. This *sunnah* regarding ablution is rejected in Shī'ah *fiqh* and therefore unlawful to them.

[191] Ibid., p. 522.

[192] *Sūrah al-Baqarah,* 2:159. *"Those who [are entitled to] curse"* refers to the angels and the believers.

[193] *Uṣūl al-Kāfī,* p. 484.

religion of Allāh, just as Prophet Yūsuf said to his brothers that they were thieves, although [he knew] they were not thieves.'"[194]

Imām Ja'far aṣ-Ṣādiq said: "Associate with your enemies outwardly and oppose them inwardly."[195]

Compare this concept with Allāh's words:

﴿يَا أَيُّهَا الَّذِينَ آمَنُوا لِمَ تَقُولُونَ مَا لاَ تَفعَلُونَ. كَبُرَ مَقتًا عِندَ اللهِ أَن تَقُولُوا مَا لاَ تَفعَلُونَ﴾

"O you who have believed, why do you say what you do not do? Great is hatred in the sight of Allāh that you say what you do not do."[196]

﴿وَلاَ تَلبِسُوا الحَقَّ بِالبَاطِلِ وَتَكتُمُوا الحَقَّ وَأَنتُم تَعلَمُونَ﴾

"And do not mix the truth with falsehood or conceal the truth while you know [it]."[197]

And still more Shī'ah narrations regarding *taqiyyah*:

Imām Ja'far aṣ-Ṣādiq said: "One who exposes something from our religion is like one who intentionally kills it."[198]

Imām Ja'far aṣ-Ṣādiq said: "When 'Abdullāh bin Ubayy died the Prophet (ﷺ) went to his graveside. 'Umar asked him, 'O Prophet, did not Allāh forbid you from standing at this grave?' The Prophet (ﷺ) was silent. 'Umar

---

[194] Ibid., p. 483.
[195] Ibid., p. 244.
[196] *Sūrah aṣ-Ṣaff,* 61:2-3.
[197] *Sūrah al-Baqarah,* 2:42.
[198] *Uṣūl al-Kāfī,* p. 88.

then repeated his question. The Prophet (ﷺ) replied, 'You do not know what I supplicated for him. I asked Allāh to fill his stomach with fire, to fill his grave with fire, and to throw him in the pit of Hellfire.'" Imām Ja'far then added: "The Prophet (ﷺ) was very unhappy to have said it because 'Umar revealed his secret."[199]

Zarārah narrated: "I asked a certain question of Imām al-Bāqir, and he gave me its answer. Another person then asked the same question, and the *imām* gave him a different answer. Later, a third person asked the same question, but the *imām's* answer that time was different than the previous two answers. I then asked him, 'O son of the Messenger, the two persons who just came here to ask you questions were from Iraq and were Shī'ahs, yet you gave them contradictory answers.' The *imām* then answered, 'O Zarārah, this is good for me as well as for you, and this will help us survive and prosper.'"[200]

Abū 'Abdullāh (Imām Ja'far) said: "My father used to say, 'Nothing is more soothing to my eye than *taqiyyah.* Indeed, *taqiyyah* is a shield for the believers.'"[201]

"Imām al-Bāqir saw a Shī'ah offering his congregational prayer behind a non-Shī'ah. When the man realized that Imām al-Bāqir was aware of his undesirable act, he personally went to the *imām* and apologized to him, saying that

---

[199]Ibid., p. 99.
[200]Ibid., p. 37.
[201]Ibid., p. 37.

he had offered his prayer under the pretext of *taqiyyah.* The *imām* then said, 'You performed a most desirable act. Had you left the congregation, the angels of the earth and the heavens would have cursed you. By offering your prayer under *taqiyyah* behind a non-Shī'ah, you are not only saved from that curse but have earned blessings 700 times more than the blessings of offering your prayer alone.'"[202]

It should be noted that most of these quotations came from the book *Uṣūl al-Kāfī.* The title page of its earlier editions carried a quotation from the last Shī'ah *imām,* which read: "This book is *kāfī* [sufficient] for our Shī'ahs." *Uṣūl al-Kāfī* means "Sufficient Fundamentals." It is still regarded as the single most comprehensive and authentic book of Shī'ah doctrine and jurisprudence.

It may also be added that most of the quotations are those attributed to the Shī'ah *imāms.* Since the Shī'ah consider them divinely appointed and immune from sin, they classify their narrations as "*ḥadīth*" and put them at par with the *ḥadīth* of Prophet Muḥammad (ﷺ). They actually derive most of their religion from the narrations of their *imāms* and not the *sunnah* of the Prophet (ﷺ). This is probably due to the fact that much of the early transmission of prophetic *ḥadīth* was done by the Prophet's companions, who are despised by Shī'ahs, and later carried on by Sunni Muslims.

According to Shī'ah narrations, the doctrine in *taqiyyah* can be summarized as follows:

1. *Taqiyyah* was supposedly practiced by Prophet Muḥammad (ﷺ) and also by other prophets.
2. 'Alī practiced *taqiyyah* for twenty-four years, pretending allegiance to the first three caliphs of Islām. Because of

---

202 *Tafseer al-'Askarī Tabriz,* p. 257.

unfavorable circumstances 'Alī continued to practice *taqiyyah* even while he himself was the caliph and *imām* of the Muslim *ummah.*

3. The Shī'ah *imāms* practiced *taqiyyah* even with their own followers. According to them, nine tenths of religion is *taqiyyah.*
4. One who does not practice *taqiyyah* has no faith and shall meet with Allāh's disgrace and punishment. Observing *taqiyyah,* on the other hand, serves as a shield against disbelief and the wrath of Allāh.

TAQIYYAH AND ISLĀMIC SHARĪ'AH

The Shī'ahs base their belief in *taqiyyah* on the following Qur'ānic verse:

﴿لاَ يَتَّخِذِ الْمُؤْمِنُونَ الْكَافِرِينَ أَوْلِيَاءَ مِن دُونِ الْمُؤْمِنِينَ وَمَن يَفْعَلْ ذَٰلِكَ فَلَيْسَ مِنَ اللهِ فِي شَيْءٍ إِلاَّ أَن تَتَّقُوا مِنْهُمْ تُقَاةً وَيُحَذِّرُكُمُ اللهُ نَفْسَهُ وَإِلَى اللهِ الْمَصِيرُ﴾

"Let not believers take as supporters disbelievers rather than believers. And whoever does that has nothing [of support] from Allāh, except by way of precaution as protection from them. And Allāh warns you of Himself, and to Allāh is the [final] destination."[203]

This verse was revealed during the early period of the Prophet's mission in Makkah. The plight of newly converted Muslims during this period was appalling. They were few in number and most were poor, weak and helpless. They were surrounded by a hostile society and had no escape from the constant harassment and persecution of the disbelievers. They were subjected to such extreme and ruthless physical torture that some of them lost their lives. It was during this critical

---

[203] *Sūrah Āli 'Imrān,* 3:28.

period that Allāh permitted the believers to use precaution to save themselves from torture by the Quraysh.

The verse in question has no relevance to the Shī'ah concept of *taqiyyah* as a way of life. Moreover, history bears witness to the fact that none of the early believers in Makkah concealed the truth about their religion. For thirteen long years the Prophet's companions lived under hardships which compelled them to leave their families, abandon their homes, and sacrifice all of their worldly belongings. Yet, not a single companion practiced *taqiyyah* under these circumstances.

If one were to believe the Shī'ah version of the meaning of this verse, it would raise basic questions about the role and conduct of the Prophet (ﷺ). If *taqiyyah* had been an option, why did he endure so much difficulty in Makkah for thirteen long years? Why did he endure the total social and economic boycott of himself and his family members for three years? Why did he engage in so many battles with the disbelievers in which some of his family members and many companions were killed? Why did he abandon his tribe, leave his home in Makkah, and emigrate to al-Madīnah? How would Shī'ahs explain the fact that the Prophet (ﷺ), according to their *imām's* narration, practiced *taqiyyah* only once (while praying for a dead hypocrite) but never practiced it in any other phase of his life?

Furthermore, such an interpretation raises basic questions about the integrity and conduct of the Shī'ah *imāms.* If 'Alī had offered allegiance to the first three caliphs for twenty-four years under the pretext of *taqiyyah,* why did al-Ḥusayn not offer a similar allegiance to Yazeed, thus saving his life and that of his family members? Did he not really understand the meaning of the "*taqiyyah*" verse? Or was he unaware that his father, 'Alī, had practiced *taqiyyah* for a period of twenty-four years?!

Again, it seems that Shī'ahs have interpreted the Qur'ān in a way as to justify their practice of *taqiyyah.* The Shī'ahs are compelled to uphold the doctrine of *taqiyyah* because its elimination would cause the entire Shī'ah religion to collapse. Likewise, the sincerity of 'Alī's allegiance to the first three caliphs could no longer be doubted, and thus the legitimacy of the caliphate would be confirmed. That, in turn, would destroy the Shī'ah myth of divinely appointed *imāms,* and then there would be no Shī'ah religion.

THE REPUTE OF 'ALĪ AND TAQIYYAH

Among the arguments advanced by Shī'ahs of their practice of *taqiyyah* is their contention that 'Alī did so when offering his allegiance to the first three caliphs. This contention should be examined in light of 'Alī's sayings and personal conduct.

During the Prophet's lifetime 'Alī engaged in numerous battles as a soldier and as a commander. During his caliphate he engaged in three major battles. He was well known for his unparalleled bravery and valor, never compromised, and always fought for what was right. Reason and logic demand that if the first three caliphs had usurped his right by deceit, he would have stood firm for justice and fought for it if necessary. It is difficult to accept that 'Alī fought for truth twenty-three years with the Prophet (ﷺ), then practiced *taqiyyah* for twenty-four years during the rule of the three caliphs, and finally reverted to fighting for truth during the six years of his own caliphate.

The contention that 'Alī practiced *taqiyyah* to preserve Muslim unity and save the *ummah* from unnecessary bloodshed is also easily refutable. The three major battles that 'Alī fought during his caliphate were those of al-Jamal, Ṣiffeen and an-Nahrwān. These battles were fought against rival Muslim groups and resulted in the death of about 10,000 Muslims. Consequently, the Muslim *ummah* was divided into four factions; one that supported 'Alī, one that opposed him, one that considered both sides to be wrong, and the majority of

Muslims who detached themselves from the conflict. It is only logical that if 'Alī had practiced *taqiyyah* with the first three caliphs to preserve the unity of the *ummah* and avoid bloodshed, he would have continued to do so for the same reason.

The majority of Muslims consider that to associate 'Alī with deception is extremely derogatory. They cannot perceive that the one who was personally trained and educated by the Prophet (ﷺ) could be so cowardly and compromising as to offer his allegiance to Abū Bakr, then to 'Umar and then to 'Uthmān under the pretext of *taqiyyah* and by so doing misguide all those who considered him a role model. The following quotations from both Shī'ah and Sunni sources illustrate 'Alī's true regard for the first three caliphs and further refute the Shī'ah position:

> *'Alī said: "When the Prophet (ﷺ) died, I accepted the temporal leadership of the one whom the Prophet (ﷺ) appointed as our imām [i.e., Abū Bakr]. We thus offered our allegiance to him."*[204]

> *When Abū Bakr tried to excuse himself from acceptance of the caliphate, 'Alī and az-Zubayr are reported to have said: "Indeed, we consider Abū Bakr as the most worthy of it after the Messenger of Allāh (ﷺ). He was [his] companion in the cave, the second of the two,*[205] *and indeed, we recognize his honor and his seniority. And the Messenger of Allāh (ﷺ) certainly ordered him to [lead] the people in prayer while he was alive."*[206]

---

[204] Al-Bukhārī.

[205] As mentioned in the Qur'ān (9:40), Abū Bakr had accompanied the Prophet (ﷺ) in his *hijrah* (emigration).

[206] Al-Ḥākim and al-Bayhaqī.

'Alī said: "The best of people after the Messenger of Allāh (ﷺ) is Abū Bakr, and the best of people after Abū Bakr is 'Umar."[207]

Ibn 'Abbās reported: "I was standing among some people, and we were supplicating Allāh for 'Umar bin al-Khaṭṭāb (may Allāh be pleased with him) after he had been placed on his bed [after death]. A man behind me put his elbow on my shoulder and [addressing 'Umar] said, 'May Allāh have mercy upon you. I am hoping that Allāh will place you with your two companions because I often used to hear the Messenger of Allāh (ﷺ) say, "I, Abū Bakr and 'Umar were [somewhere]" or "I, Abū Bakr and 'Umar did [something]" or "I set out with Abū Bakr and 'Umar" – so I am hoping that Allāh will place you with them.' I turned and found that it was 'Alī bin Abī Ṭālib [speaking], may Allāh be pleased with him."[208]

'Alī loved and respected 'Umar so much that he married his daughter Umm Kulthūm to him. Umm Kulthūm's mother was Fāṭimah, Prophet Muḥammad's daughter. This marriage is recorded in both Sunni and Shī'ah sources, but the Shī'ahs claim that 'Alī only married his daughter to 'Umar under the pretext of *taqiyyah.*

The following quotations show the great care and respect that 'Alī held for 'Umar:

"When 'Umar became caliph, 'Alī began calling him *Ameer al-Mu'mineen* [Leader of the Believers]."[209]

---

[207] Ibn Mājah.
[208] Al-Bukhārī. Muslim related similar words from Ibn 'Abbās.
[209] *Sharḥ Nahj al-Balāghah,* vol. 2.

> "When 'Umar became caliph, 'Alī stayed close to him and counseled him on various important occasions. During the invasion of Persia when 'Umar wanted to lead the army personally, he consulted 'Alī, who said to him, 'The success or failure of Islām is not dependent upon the number of soldiers. The position of caliph is like that which connects all the beads in a necklace. If this connection is removed, all the beads are scattered. You are like the needle of a compass for the believers. If you are gone [to the battlefield], various tribes might invade Madīnah. Furthermore, if the Persians see you in the battlefield, they will say, "Here is the leader of the Arabs; if you kill him, you will have peace." We, the companions of the Prophet (ﷺ), never fought our enemy with large numbers during the Prophet's lifetime. Now, at the present time as well, you should trust in the blessing of Allāh and fight the Persians by staying in Madīnah.'"[210]

'Alī so loved and respected the first three caliphs that he named his sons after them. According to two famous Shī'ah books, *Kashf al-Ghummah* and *Jalāl al-'Ayūn,* the names of 'Alī's fourteen sons are: al-Ḥasan, al-Ḥusayn, Muḥammad al-Akbar, 'Abdullāh, Abū Bakr, al-'Abbās, 'Uthmān, Ja'far, 'Ubaydullāh, Muḥammad al-Aṣghar, Yaḥyā, 'Aun, 'Umar, and Muḥammad al-Awsaṭ.

The preceding quotations from both authentic Sunni and Shī'ah sources speak of 'Alī's respect for the caliphs who preceded him. Marrying his daughter to 'Umar and naming his sons after Abū Bakr, 'Umar, and 'Uthmān in particular are open testimonies to his feelings. If all this was done out of

---

[210] *Nairung Fasāḥat,* p. 22.

taqiyyah, it seems that he would have declared the truth once he himself became head of the Muslim state, but history bears witness to the fact that even after 'Alī became caliph, he neither denounced the previous caliphs, called them usurpers of his right, or disassociated himself from their general practices.

It should also be pointed out that even if 'Alī for some hypothetical motive had been forced to continue *taqiyyah,* there was no reason whatsoever for him to practice it with his own followers and close family members, and he could have at least revealed the names of the *imāms* who would succeed him. Had he done so, the second *imām,* al-Ḥasan, could not have abdicated his right in favor of Mu'āwiyah.

A total of sixty-five different descendants of 'Alī later claimed to be divinely appointed *imāms,* fought for their claims and were ultimately killed.[211] Shī'ahs are still divided into sects, each group claiming a different set of *imāms.* This is due to the Shī'ah belief that because 'Alī practiced *taqiyyah,* he did not reveal the names of his successors. Shī'ahs have explained a major portion of 'Alī's conduct as *taqiyyah* – to the extent that there remains no difference between *taqiyyah* and hypocrisy. It is a well-known fact that there were many in Madīnah who professed Islām, prayed and participated in *jihād,* yet the Qur'ān calls them hypocrites because their intention was to deceive. How, one wonders, do Shī'ahs differentiate between 'Alī and those hypocrites of Madīnah?

In conclusion, reason, common sense, and above all, recorded history, leads one to the certainty that 'Alī did not practice *taqiyyah* at any stage of his life. All his sayings, writings, and the accounts of his personal and public conduct confirm his uncompromising integrity. He was one of the companions most knowledgeable about Islām and personally trained by the Prophet (ﷺ), who thus served as a role model

---

211 *Ṭabaqāt Ibn Sa'd,* vol. 8, p. 10.

for his contemporaries and all generations to follow. He offered a true and sincere allegiance to the first three caliphs and thereby affirmed the legitimacy of the caliphate. Recorded history does not offer a single evidence that 'Alī claimed to be a divinely appointed *imām* or that the imamate would be reserved for his progeny. Shī'ahs have had to invent the doctrine of *taqiyyah* in order to assert something that was never evident in the exemplary conduct of 'Alī.

THE SHĪ'AH IMĀMS[212] AND TAQIYYAH

It would also be appropriate to refer to sources of Islāmic history to ascertain whether or not the Shī'ah *imāms* actually practiced *taqiyyah.* All authentic Sunni sources and most Shī'ah books concede that the *imāms* ('Alī's descendants) showed utmost love and respect for the first three caliphs and considered them to be the legitimate *imāms* of the Muslim *ummah.* Below are a few quotations which illustrate this. Preceding pages have already mentioned the regard of 'Alī for the other three caliphs.

- The Shī'ah's Second Imām: al-Ḥasan bin 'Alī

> *Al-Ḥasan reported that the Prophet* (ﷺ) *said: "Abū Bakr is for me [like] my ears, 'Umar [like] my eyes, and 'Uthmān [like] my heart."*[213]

Al-Ḥasan had eight sons and named two of them after the first caliphs. Their names are al-Ḥasan, Zayd, 'Umar, al-Qāsim, Abū Bakr, Ṭalḥah, 'Abdur-Raḥmān and 'Ubaydullāh.[214]

---

[212] Neither 'Alī nor his direct descendants considered themselves anything but Muslims and certainly not propagators of any sect or separate religious creed. It is the Shī'ahs who consider them as their own religious leaders, attributing to them many inconceivable narrations to support their doctrines.

[213] *Ṭabaqāt Ibn Sa'd,* vol. 8, p. 10.

[214] *Tareekh al-Ya'qūbī,* vol. 4, p. 179.

◆ The Shī'ah's Third Imām: al-Ḥusayn bin 'Alī

Al-Ḥusayn had several sons. History records that he named two of them Abū Bakr and 'Umar.

◆ The Shī'ah's Fourth Imām: 'Alī Zayn al-Abideen bin al-Ḥusayn

> "Abū Ṣafar said that Zayn al-Abideen frequently used [to wrap himself in] a certain sheet. Someone asked him the reason for using that sheet so frequently. He replied, 'This is the sheet that my sincere, beloved, kind and compassionate friend, 'Umar, wrapped around my body. Indeed, 'Umar was a great servant of Allāh. May Allāh be pleased with him.' The narrator added that Zayn al-Abideen began to weep while saying these words."[215]

◆ The Shī'ah's Fifth Imām: Muḥammad al-Bāqir

> Imām al-Bāqir said: "One who is not aware of the virtues of Abū Bakr is ignorant of the *sunnah* on the noble Prophet (ﷺ)."[216]

> *"When Imām Abū Ḥanīfah went to Madīnah, he asked Muḥammad al-Bāqir his opinion about Abū Bakr and 'Umar. Al-Bāqir replied, 'May Allāh be pleased with them.' Abū Ḥanīfah told him that there was a common belief in 'Irāq that he [i.e., Imām al-Bāqir] had disassociated himself from these persons. He replied, 'May Allāh protect me! By the Lord of the Ka'bah, they tell a lie.' He then reminded Abū Ḥanīfah of 'Umar's marriage to Umm Kulthūm, the daughter of 'Alī and Fāṭimah, and*

---

[215] Ibid., vol. 2, p. 228.
[216] *'Ilal Ibn Abī Shaybah,* vol. 4, p. 179.

asked him, 'How could have 'Alī given his daughter [in marriage] to 'Umar if he was not worthy of this marriage?' Abū Ḥanīfah then said, 'Why do you not put his down in writing and send it to [the Shī'ahs of] 'Irāq?' To this al-Bāqir said, 'They will not accept my writing.'"[217]

Jābir reported: "I asked al-Bāqir, 'Has there ever been among the Prophet's family members a group which denounced Abū Bakr and 'Umar?' He replied, 'No, I myself love both of them, respect them and pray that Allāh be pleased with them.'"[218]

◆ The Shī'ah's Sixth Imām: Ja'far aṣ-Ṣādiq

"Someone informed Imām Ja'far aṣ-Ṣādiq that a certain person thought that he [i.e., Ja'far] detested and denounced Abū Bakr and 'Umar. Ja'far replied, 'I have nothing to do with this person. Rather, I hope that my relationship with Abū Bakr may bring blessings upon my family.'"[219]

Ja'far aṣ-Ṣādiq said: "Abū Bakr is my grandfather. Would someone like to curse and denounce his own forefathers? May Allāh deprive me of all respect and honor if I do not acknowledge with respect and reverence the dignity of aṣ-Ṣiddeeq [i.e., Abū Bakr]."[220]

---

217 *Aṣ-Ṣawā'iq al-Muḥarriqah,* p. 28.
218 *Ṭabaqāt Ibn Sa'd,* p. 236.
219 *Ar-Riyādh an-Nathirah,* vol. 1, p. 59.
220 *Iḥqāq al-Ḥaqq,* p. 7.

◆ The Shī'ah's Ninth Imām: Muḥammad at-Taqī

> At-Taqī said: "I do not deny the virtue of 'Umar, but Abū Bakr is superior to 'Umar."[221]

The above quotations from both Sunni and Shī'ah sources show that 'Alī's descendants, whom the Shī'ah's consider to be their divinely appointed *imāms,* also acknowledged the righteousness and piety of the first three caliphs. Moreover, they believed in the legitimacy of their caliphate. Since the Shī'ahs cannot deny the authenticity of their own source books, they would logically be expected to revert to their doctrine of *taqiyyah* and say that all their *imāms* also practiced *taqiyyah.* In fact, *taqiyyah* has provided the great shield of escape for all Shī'ah inconsistencies. It is for this reason that they have said that nine tenths of their religion is *taqiyyah.*

It has been shown that the righteous conduct of 'Alī and the other *imāms* takes on a different meaning under the guise of *taqiyyah.* Shī'ahs are thus hard pressed to uphold the doctrine of *taqiyyah* in order to reject the legitimacy of the first three caliphs and justify the imamate of 'Alī's descendants. In truth, neither 'Alī nor his direct descendants knew anything of Shī'ism as it is today and would surely have condemned it had they known. Having begun as a political movement, it took several generations for this particular creed to develop. Only by blemishing the reputations of 'Alī and his descendants, attributing to them the practice of *taqiyyah,* can they claim them as their own religious leaders.

---

[221] *Al-Iḥtijāj 'alā Ahl al-Lajāj,* p. 250.

THE PRACTICE OF MUT'AH (TEMPORARY MARRIAGE)

Mut'ah is an Arabic word which means "enjoyment" and to Shī'ahs has a deep religious connotation. The books of "*ḥadīth*" and *fiqh* written by Shī'ah scholars define *mut'ah* as "a temporary marriage contracted for a fixed period in return for a compensation." The belief in the sanctity and merits of *mut'ah* is an integral part of Shī'ah faith. In contrast, the rest of the Muslim *ummah* considers *mut'ah* as little more than prostitution.

Shī'ahs justify their belief in *mut'ah* with the following verse from the Qur'ān, and they claim that this verse was revealed specifically to declare the sanctity of *mut'ah*:

﴿وَالْمُحصَنَاتُ مِنَ النِّسَاءِ إِلاَّ مَا مَلَكَت أَيـمَانُكُم كِتَابَ اللهِ عَلَيكُم وَأُحِلَّ لَكُم مَا وَرَاءَ ذَلِكُم أَن تَبتَغُوا بِأَموَالِكُم مُحصِنِينَ غَيرَ مُسَافِحِينَ فَمَا استَمتَعتُم بِهِ مِنهُنَّ فَآتُوهُنَّ أُجُورَهُنَّ فَرِيضَةً﴾

"And [prohibited to you are all] married women except those your right hands possess. [This is] the decree of Allāh upon you. And lawful to you are [all others] beyond these, [provided] that you seek them [in marriage] with [gifts from] your property, desiring chastity, not unlawful sexual intercourse. So for whatever you enjoy [of marriage] from them, give them their due compensation[222] *as an obligation."*[223]

The Shī'ahs claim that *mut'ah* was openly practiced during the Prophet's lifetime and that it was only the second caliph, 'Umar, who forcefully prohibited this practice. They even go to the extent of saying:

---

[222] The *mahr,* a specified gift to the bride required of the man upon marriage.

[223] *Sūrah an-Nisā',* 4:24.

"The believer is perfect only when he has experienced *mut'ah*."[224]

Sunnis acknowledge that *mut'ah* was a common practice during the pre-Islāmic days of ignorance (*jāhiliyyah*) in Arabia. It is stated in at-Tirmidhī's book of *ḥadīth* in the chapter on marriage that when a man would go to a strange village where he had no acquaintance, he would marry a woman for as long a period as he thought that he would stay there so that she could take care of him and his property. This practice continued during the early days of Islām until Allāh revealed among verses describing the believers:

﴿وَالَّذِينَ هُم لِفُرُوجِهِم حَافِظُونَ. إِلاَّ عَلَى أَزوَاجِهِم أَو مَا مَلَكَت أَيمَانُهُم﴾

"...And they who guard their private parts except from their wives or those their right hands possess..."[225]

The *Shorter Encyclopaedia of Islam* also states that *mut'ah* was a common practice among Arab travelers and goes back to the fourth century A.D. "When a stranger came to a village and had no place to stay, he would marry a woman for a short time so that she would be his partner in bed and take care of his property." Caetani also stated that in the pagan period *mut'ah* was a form of religious prostitution that took place during the occasion of *ḥajj*.[226]

Thus, *mut'ah* was a loose sexual practice during the pre-Islāmic days of ignorance in Arabia. Being an old and established institution, it continued during the early days of Islām. The Prophet (ﷺ) also allowed it temporarily on two other occasions, but only under strict, exceptional conditions –

---

224 *Shorter Encyclopaedia of Islam,* p. 419.
225 *Sūrah al-Mu'minūn,* 23:5-6.
226 *Shorter Encyclopaedia of Islam,* p. 419.

during the conquest of Khaybar and during the conquest of Makkah – fearing that those Muslims whose faith was not yet strong might commit adultery during *jihād.* Shī'ahs widely quote *ḥadīths* in relation to these events to support their continued belief in *mut'ah.* Sunnis accept these *ḥadīths* but add that this happened before all of the verses of the Qur'ān were revealed and the religion completed.

Historians and commentators on the Qur'ān and *ḥadīth* agree that Islām eradicated most social evils in a gradual way. It is well known that practices like gambling, drinking, and consumption of pork and blood were common during the early days but were prohibited gradually. Likewise, it is probable that *mut'ah* was first forbidden to those at Khaybar in the year 7 A.H. and then completely prohibited to all people upon the conquest of Makkah in 8 A.H.

Several *ḥadīths* of the Prophet (ﷺ) regarding *mut'ah* are well documented, such as the following:

> *'Alī reported: "On the day of the conquest of Khaybar the Prophet (ﷺ) forbade mut'ah and [eating] the flesh of a donkey."*[227]

> *Sabrah bin Ma'bad al-Juhanī reported: "I went forth with the Prophet (ﷺ) for the conquest of Makkah, and he allowed us mut'ah with women. But we had not even left the city [yet] when it was prohibited by the Messenger of Allāh (ﷺ)."*[228]

According to al-Bayhaqī, Ja'far aṣ-Ṣādiq, the sixth Shī'ah *imām,* regarded *mut'ah* as fornication.[229] And 'Alī is reported by ad-Dārquṭnī to have said that *mut'ah* was abrogated when the Qur'ānic verses about marriage, divorce, *'iddah,*[230] and

---

227 *Ṣaḥeeḥ Muslim.*

228 Ibid.

229 *Fatḥ ul-Bāri,* p. 173.

230 The mandatory period of waiting before a widowed or divorced woman can remarry.

inheritance were revealed.[231] Additionally, there are four *ḥadīths* quoted in *Ṣaḥeeḥ al-Bukhārī* under the title "The Prophet Finally Forbade Mut'ah." Three of these relate to the incidents of *mut'ah* during the early period of Islām. In the fourth *ḥadīth* 'Alī said to Ibn 'Abbās that the Prophet (ﷺ) forbade *mut'ah* and the meat of domesticated donkeys on the day of Khaybar. And in *Ṣaḥeeḥ Muslim* a group of traditions which go back to Sabrah bin Ma'bad substantiate that the Prophet (ﷺ) permitted *mut'ah* in the year of the conquest of Makkah. Sabrah went with a companion to a woman, and each offered her a cloak in exchange for *mut'ah*. She chose the younger person with a shabbier cloak (i.e., Sabrah) and slept with him for three nights. Thereafter, Sabrah related, the Prophet (ﷺ) forbade it forever.

A Shī'ah might object to the aforementioned information because it is from Sunni sources. The fact is, however, that the Qur'ān itself negates the Shī'ah concept of *mut'ah*. First, the verse Shī'ahs present in support of *mut'ah* should be examined. The last part of the verse reads:

﴿وَأُحِلَّ لَكُم مَا وَرَاءَ ذَٰلِكُم أَن تَبتَغُوا بِأَموَالِكُم مُحصِنِينَ غَيرَ مُسَافِحِينَ فَمَا استَمتَعتُم بِهِ مِنهُنَّ فَآتُوهُنَّ أُجُورَهُنَّ فَرِيضَةً﴾

> *"And lawful to you are [all others] beyond these, [provided] that you seek them [in marriage] with [gifts from] your property, desiring chastity, not unlawful sexual intercourse. So for whatever you enjoy [of marriage] from them, give them their due compensation as an obligation."*[232]

This verse clearly emphasizes the concept of chastity through legal marriage. *Mut'ah*, on the other hand, is an open

---

231 *Muta*, p. 11.
232 *Sūrah an-Nisā'*, 4:24.

license for sexual pleasure with as many women as one can financially afford. The women who engage in *mut'ah* are hired women; thus, it can be performed with any woman irrespective of her age, character, conduct or religion. It requires no witnesses, nor is there any obligation on the man's part to provide food and shelter for the woman, not to speak of a child born of the relationship. The only precondition is that the woman agrees to the price and the length of the *mut'ah* and that the man pays her the compensation when he has relations with her. One can discern for himself whether such a practice would promote chastity or lead to sheer promiscuity.

Two terms in the verse under discussion are used by Shī'ah commentators to support the permissibility of *mut'ah.* The first word is "*ujūr*" (pl. of *ajr*), which means "compensation"; the second is "*istamta'tum,*" which can be translated as "what you have enjoyed." So the end of the verse could be translated: "But give them their compensation for what you have enjoyed of them [in keeping with your promise]." Shī'ah commentators claim that "*ajr*" refers to the price of *mut'ah* agreed upon by the two parties, while Sunnis uphold that it refers to the *mahr* (a bridal gift given by the husband to the wife in a legal marriage). Similarly, Shī'ahs explain the term "*istamta'tum*" as the physical act of consummation. However, this is invalidated by the use of the same word in other Qur'ānic verses:

﴿فَاسْتَمْتَعُوا بِخَلَاقِهِم فَاسْتَمْتَعْتُم بِخَلَاقِكُم كَمَا اسْتَمْتَعَ الَّذِينَ مِن قَبْلِكُم﴾

"They had enjoyment [fastamta'ū] *of their portion [of worldly life], and you have had enjoyment* [fastamta'tum] *of yours as those before you enjoyed* [istamta'a] *theirs."*[233]

[233] *Sūrah at-Tawbah,* 9:69.

﴿وَقَالَ أَوْلِيَاؤُهُم مِنَ الإِنسِ رَبَّنَا اسْتَمْتَعَ بَعْضُنَا بِبَعْضٍ وَبَلَغْنَا أَجَلَنَا﴾

"Their friends among men will say, 'Our Lord, we enjoyed [astamta'a] *each other but have reached our term."*[234]

﴿وَيَوْمَ يُعْرَضُ الَّذِينَ كَفَرُوا عَلَى النَّارِ أَذْهَبْتُمْ طَيِّبَاتِكُمْ فِي حَيَاتِكُمُ الدُّنْيَا وَاسْتَمْتَعْتُم بِهَا﴾

"And on the Day that the disbelievers will be placed before fire, [it will be said to them], 'You used up your good things in the life of this world and enjoyed [wastamta'tum] *them.'"*[235]

The aforementioned Qur'ānic verses contain different forms of this same word. Yet, none of them gives a hint of the meaning interpreted by the Shī'ahs. In fact, Shī'ahs do not relate any of these verses to the their concept of *mut'ah.*

Other verses of the Qur'ān contain derivatives of the root (م ت ع) which comprises the word "*mut'ah*" (literally, "enjoyment"), such as "*tamatta'a*" ("to enjoy") and "*matta'a*" ("to give enjoyment"). For example:

﴿أَفَرَأَيْتَ إِن مَّتَّعْنَاهُمْ سِنِينَ. ثُمَّ جَاءَهُم مَّا كَانُوا يُوعَدُونَ. مَا أَغْنَى عَنْهُم مَّا كَانُوا يُمَتَّعُونَ﴾

"So have you considered if We gave them enjoyment [matta'nāhum] *for years and then there came to them that which they were promised? They would not be availed by that which they were given to enjoy* [yumatta'ūn]. *"*[236]

---

[234] *Sūrah al-An'ām,* 6:128.
[235] *Sūrah al-Aḥqāf,* 46:20.
[236] *Sūrah ash-Shu'arā',* 26:205-207.

﴿نُمَتِّعُهُم قَلِيلاً ثُمَّ نَضطَرُّهُم إِلَى عَذَابٍ غَلِيظٍ﴾

"We grant them enjoyment [numatti'uhum] *for a little; then We will force them to a harsh punishment."*[237]

Any claim that this word, designating enjoyment or provision in a general sense, carries a specific connotation in connection with marriage can easily be refuted by presenting other verses which not only deal with the subject in question but contain the same derivatives. These are as follows:

﴿لاَ جُنَاحَ عَلَيكُم إِن طَلَّقتُمُ النِّسَاءَ مَا لَم تَمَسُّوهُنَّ أَو تَفرِضُوا لَهُنَّ فَرِيضَةً وَمَتِّعُوهُنَّ عَلَى المُوسِعِ قَدَرُهُ وَعَلَى المُقتِرِ قَدَرُهُ مَتَاعًا بِالمَعرُوفِ حَقًّا عَلَى المُحسِنِينَ﴾

"There is no blame upon you if you have divorced women whom you have not touched [i.e., the marriage has not been consummated] or specified for them an obligation [i.e., mahr]. But give them [a gift of] compensation [matti'ūhunna]. *The wealthy has his capability and the poor has his capability – a provision* [matā'an] *according to what is acceptable, an obligation upon the righteous."*[238]

﴿يَا أَيُّهَا النَّبِيُّ قُل لِأَزوَاجِكَ إِن كُنتُنَّ تُرِدنَ الحَيَاةَ الدُّنيَا وَزِينَتَهَا فَتَعَالَينَ أُمَتِّعكُنَّ وَأُسَرِّحكُنَّ سَرَاحًا جَمِيلاً﴾

"O Prophet, say to your wives, 'If you desire the life of this world and its glitter, then come, I will provide for you [umatti'kunna] *and set you free in a handsome manner."*[239]

---

237 *Sūrah Luqmān,* 31:24.
238 *Sūrah al-Baqarah,* 2:236.
239 *Sūrah al-Aḥzāb,* 33:28.

﴿يَا أَيُّهَا الَّذِينَ آمَنُوا إِذَا نَكَحتُمُ الـمُؤمِنَاتِ ثُـمَّ طَلَّقتُمُوهُـنَّ مِـن قَبلِ أَن تَمَسُّوهُنَّ فَمَالَكُم عَلَيهِـنَّ مِـن عِـدَّةٍ تَعتَدُّونَهَـا فَمَتِّعُوهُـنَّ وَسَرِّحُوهُنَّ سَرَاحًا جَمِيلاً﴾

"O you who have believed, when you marry believing women and then divorce them before you have touched them, no period of waiting have you to count in respect to them. So give them provision [matti'ūhunna] *and set them free in a handsome manner."*[240]

Thus, a careful examination of the term "*istamta'a*" and related words throughout the Qur'ān shows that there is no basis for an assumption that in verse 4:24 there is a reference to temporary marriage. This is further clarified by the verse which follows it, one which the Shī'ahs have chosen to ignore:

﴿فَانكِحُوهُنَّ بِـإِذنِ أَهلِهِنَّ وَآتُوهُنَّ أُجُورَهُنَّ بِالـمَعرُوفِ﴾

"So marry them with the permission of their people and give them their due compensation according to what is reasonable."[241]

Despite the fact that this verse deals with marriage to slaves, the reference is obviously to a regular legal marriage since permission is not necessary in *mut'ah.* While Shī'ahs prefer their own interpretation of a single verse over all evidence to the contrary, the Muslim *ummah* unanimously upholds that *mut'ah* has been abrogated by all of the Qur'ānic verses that speak about marriage, divorce, inheritance, dower, the guardian's permission, the *'iddah* of divorced and widowed women, etc.

Additionally, the following verse describing the believers leaves no doubt that *mut'ah* is unlawful to them:

---

240 *Sūrah al-Aḥzāb,* 33:49.
241 *Sūrah an-Nisā',* 4:25.

﴿وَالَّذِينَ هُمْ لِفُرُوجِهِمْ حَافِظُونَ. إِلاَّ عَلَى أَزْوَاجِهِمْ أَوْ مَا مَلَكَتْ أَيْمَانُهُمْ﴾

"...And they who guard their private parts except from their wives or those their right hands possess..."[242]

Explaining these words, Ibn 'Abbās said, "All other ways of sexual contact except these two are forbidden."[243]

As mentioned earlier, Shī'ahs claim that it was 'Umar who forbade the practice of *mut'ah* and that *mut'ah* was practiced openly during the lifetimes of the Prophet (ﷺ) and Abū Bakr. Sunnis acknowledge that 'Umar again[244] declared *mut'ah* to be illegal, but they add that he did not initiate the ruling himself. 'Umar was elected caliph just two and a half years after the Prophet's death. Around him were the respected family members and companions of the Prophet (ﷺ). Had 'Umar's declaration been contrary to the Prophet's practice, a number of those noble people would certainly have objected to it. Yet, nowhere in Islāmic history is recorded a single protest against his announcement. Furthermore, since 'Umar was later succeeded by 'Uthmān and then by 'Alī, had 'Umar's statement been contrary to the ruling of the Prophet (ﷺ), at least one of them should have reestablished the practice of *mut'ah.* Again, there are no records of such a revision. Oddly enough, in the voluminous book, *Nahj al-Balāghah* (said to be a collection of 'Alī's sermons and other sayings wherein he presented various aspects of Islām and the Muslim state), not a single word in favor of *mut'ah* was mentioned. Had 'Umar been wrong, nothing would have prevented 'Alī from condemning it. The fact is that from the time of the Prophet's death there has been a consensus within the Muslim *ummah*

---

242 *Sūrah al-Mu'minūn,* 23:5-6.

243 *Tafseer* related by at-Tirmidhī.

244 After the initial prohibitions of the Prophet (ﷺ).

about the illegality of *mut'ah.* Some people were apparently unaware of its prohibition and may have contracted it after the Prophet's death. Consequently, when 'Umar knew of it, he made a further public declaration against *mut'ah* and enforced the ruling in his capacity as caliph and head of the Islāmic state.

THE CONCEPT OF MUT'AH AS EXPLAINED BY SHĪ'AH SOURCES

The following citations from the most recognized sources of Shī'ah beliefs and practices elaborate on the concept of *mut'ah.* They need to be presented that one may determine whether *mut'ah* promotes chastity, as desired by Almighty Allāh, or exactly the opposite.

◆ Women Eligible for Mut'ah

> "*Mut'ah* is allowed with all types of women. She may be a virgin, married, widowed or may belong to any sect, group or religion. She may be a Christian, Jew or Muslim. However, *mut'ah* with a Majūsī [Magian] woman is permissible only when one is helpless."[245]
>
> Zarārah said: "I asked the *imām* [i.e., Ja'far aṣ-Ṣādiq] with how many different girls one can contract *mut'ah.* He answered, 'With as many as one likes. These women are like hired girls.'"[246]
>
> "If one desires, he may have *mut'ah* with one thousand women since these are like hired women."[247]

---

245 *Tahdheeb al-Aḥkām,* p. 188.
246 *Furu' al-Kāfī,* vol. 2, p. 191.
247 *Tahdheeb al-Aḥkām,* p. 188.

"The narrator asked Imām Ja'far aṣ-Ṣādiq, 'In al-Kūfah there is a woman known for her dubious character. Can I engage in *mut'ah* with her?' The *imām* said, 'Yes, you may engage in *mut'ah* with her.'"[248]

"Abān bin Tughlaq related that he said to Imām Ja'far aṣ-Ṣādiq, 'Often during my travels I come across a very beautiful woman and am not sure if she has a husband or if she is an adulteress or if she is one of dubious character.' The *imām* responded, 'Why should you worry about all of these things? Your duty is to believe what she says. If she says that she has no husband, then you should engage in *mut'ah* with her.'"[249]

"Jameel bin ad-Dārī said that he asked Imām Ja'far aṣ-Ṣādiq if *mut'ah* was permissible with a virgin girl. The *imām* said, 'There is no harm in it if the girl is not too young. However, all of the collectors of *ḥadīth* agree that a nine-year-old girl is not considered too young.'"[250]

◆ Contracting Mut'ah

"When Hishām Sālim asked how one should contract *mut'ah,* Imām Ja'far aṣ-Ṣādiq answered that one should say, 'I am marrying you for this period of time for this amount [of money]. When the prescribed period is over, there will be annulment and no *'iddah* after that.'"[251]

---

[248]Ibid., vol. 2, p. 249.

[249]*Furu' al-Kāfī,* vol. 2, p. 196; *Tahdheeb al-Aḥkām,* p. 187.

[250]*Furu' al-Kāfī,* p. 196.

[251] *Tahdheeb al-Aḥkām,* p. 183.

"The narrator asked Imām al-Bāqir about the women of *mut'ah.* The *imām* said, 'She is not among those four [classified as wives] because she neither needs a divorce nor is entitled to any inheritance. She is like a hired woman!'"[252]

"There is no need for witnesses or any open declaration in *mut'ah.*"[253]

"One may have sexual relations with the woman contracted for *mut'ah* any number of times he desires."[254]

◆ The Price of Mut'ah

"The narrator asked Imām Ja'far aṣ-Ṣādiq, 'What should be the minimum compensation for *mut'ah*?' The *imām* said, 'Anything that the two parties agree upon.'"[255]

"*Mut'ah* is a marriage that may last for a very short time. It needs no witnesses, and it has no period of *'iddah.* The minimum compensation that could be paid to the woman for sexual relations is one *dirham.*"[256]

◆ The Merits of Mut'ah

"No one can close the door of blessings which Allāh opens for His servants. Imām Ja'far aṣ-Ṣādiq said, '*Mut'ah* is one of the blessings of Allāh.'"[257]

---

252 *Tahdheeb al-Aḥkām,* p. 188; *Man Lā Yaḥdhuruhul-Faqeeh,* p. 139; *Uṣūl al-Kāfī,* vol. 2, p. 191.

253 *Tahdheeb al-Aḥkām,* p. 189.

254 *Furu' al-Kāfī,* vol. 2, p. 195.

255 Ibid., p. 189.

256 *Furu' al-Kāfī,* vol. 2, p. 194; *Man Lā Yaḥdhuruhul-Faqeeh,* vol. 3, p. 149; *Tahdheeb al-Aḥkām,* p. 189.

257 *Tafseer al-Qummī,* p. 308.

"If a man contracts *mut'ah* once in his lifetime, Allāh will grant him Paradise."[258]

"One who contracts *mut'ah* is saved from *shirk* [the greatest sin of ascribing partners to Allāh]."[259]

"It is narrated by Imām al-Bāqir that the Prophet (ﷺ) said: 'When I was being taken to Heaven during the *Mi'rāj* (ascension), Jibreel met me and told me, "O Muḥammad, Allāh has promised to forgive all of the sins of those women who practice *mut'ah.*"'"[260]

"Imām Ja'far aṣ-Ṣādiq narrated from the Prophet (ﷺ) that one third of the body is saved from the Hellfire if one contracts *mut'ah* once. Two thirds of the body is saved if one contracts *mut'ah* twice, and the whole body is saved from Hell if one contracts *mut'ah* three times."[261]

"The Prophet (ﷺ) said: 'The man who contracts *mut'ah* once will be saved from the Hellfire. One who contracts it twice will be in the company of virtuous men [in Paradise]. And the one who contracts it three times will be my companion in *firdaws* [the highest level of Paradise].'"[262]

---

258 *Minhāj aṣ-Ṣādiqeen,* p. 356.
259 Ibid., p. 357.
260 *Man Lā Yaḥdhuruhul-Faqeeh,* p. 150. It must be noted that this and the following narrations attributed to the Prophet (ﷺ) are forged and thus must not be misconstrued as being an authentic *ḥadīth* from the *sunnah.*
261 *Minhāj aṣ-Ṣādiqeen,* p. 354.
262 Ibid., p. 356. A forged narration.

"One who engages in *mut'ah* once attains the status of Imām al-Ḥusayn. One who engages in it twice becomes equal in status to Imām al-Ḥasan. The one who performs it three times reaches the position of Imām 'Alī. And he who practices it four times acquires the level and position [equal to that] of the Prophet (ﷺ)."[263]

"It is narrated that once the Prophet (ﷺ) was sitting among his companions and the discussion came to the topic of *mut'ah.* The Prophet (ﷺ) said, 'Do you know what is the reward of *mut'ah*?' The companions answered, 'No.' The Prophet (ﷺ) then said, 'Jibreel just came to me and said, "O Muḥammad, Allāh sends His blessings to you and commands you to instruct your *ummah* to engage in the practice of *mut'ah* since this is the practice of [Allāh's] virtuous servants."'"[264]

"Abū Sālim bin 'Uqbah said that he asked Imām Ja'far aṣ-Ṣādiq if there was reward in agreeing to *mut'ah.* The *imām* said, 'Yes, if it is practiced for seeking the pleasure of Allāh and to oppose those who deny the sanctity of *mut'ah.* Thus, when a person engages in *mut'ah,* all of his private talking to the woman is recorded as merits. When he extends his arms towards the woman, this is also written as a merit. When he engages in the sexual act with the woman, Allāh forgives all of his sins. When the two take a bath, Allāh showers His blessings upon them and forgives their sins

---

[263]Ibid.
[264]Ibid.

equal to the amount of hair [on their bodies].' The narrator inquired in surprise, 'Equal to the amount of hair on their bodies?' The *imām* replied, 'Yes, for every one single hair [wet by the water]. But their reward is reduced by the amount of hair that may not be wet.'"[265]

"'Alī asked the Prophet (ﷺ), 'What is the reward of the person who participates in the virtuous deed of arranging the mutual meetings of a man and woman?' The Prophet (ﷺ) said, 'He will receive the same reward as the two who engage in *mut'ah.*'"[266]

- Denial of Mut'ah

"One who does not believe that we [i.e., the Shī'ah *imāms*] will reappear and rule [the world in the future] and one who does not believe in the sanctity of *mut'ah* is not from among us."[267]

"The Prophet (ﷺ) said: 'The men and women who die without performing *mut'ah* even once in their lives will appear on the Day of Judgement with their ears and nose cut and [their faces] deformed.'"[268]

- Reward for Women Who Return Their Payment

"For the woman who donates back her compensation to the person who contracted *mut'ah* with her and for the woman who

---

[265] *Minhāj aṣ-Ṣādiqeen,* p. 354; *Man Lā Yaḥdhuruhul-Faqeeh,* p. 150.
[266] *Minhāj aṣ-Ṣādiqeen,* p. 356. A forged *ḥadīth.*
[267] Ibid., p. 354.
[268] Ibid., p. 354. A forged *ḥadīth.*

> foregoes her dowry, Allāh will reward her with 40,000 cities of light and 70,000 dresses of velvet and silk brocade... And Allāh will reward her with 70,000 more dresses from Heaven for each quarter of a *dirham* she donates back... And for each quarter of a *dirham* Allāh will also assign 1,000 angels who will continue writing merits in her account until the Day of Judgement."[269]

Shī'ahs claim that it was Allāh and His Prophet (ﷺ) who made *mut'ah* a blessing for the Muslim *ummah.* The following citations attributed to Imām Abū 'Abdullāh Ja'far aṣ-Ṣādiq illustrate:

> "The Qur'ān was revealed to declare the sanctity of *mut'ah.* The Prophet (ﷺ) also practiced *mut'ah.*"[270]

> "Allāh has prohibited all intoxicating drinks for the Shī'ahs, but instead He has granted them *mut'ah.*"[271]

> "The Qur'ān was revealed to justify *mut'ah,* and people practiced it in accordance with the *sunnah* of the Prophet (ﷺ)."[272]

Two important points should be recalled concerning the aforementioned quotations. The alleged sayings of the Shī'ah *imāms* are classified by them as "*ḥadīths.*" Technically, Shī'ahs make no distinction between the sayings of the Prophet (ﷺ) and those of their *imāms,* which serve as the

---

269 *Tafseer al-Qummī,* p. 357.

270 *Furu' al-Kāfī,* p. 23. May Allāh forgive me for quoting such a derogatory statement about the Prophet (ﷺ) in order to preserve the objectivity of the argument.

271 *Man Lā Yaḥdhuruhul-Faqeeh,* vol. 2, p. 151.

272 *Furu' al-Kāfī,* vol. 2, p. 120.

foundation of the Shī'ah faith and practice.

The citations on preceding pages are from authentic and recognized Shī'ah sources. *Tafseer al-Qummī* and *Tafseer Minhāj aṣ-Ṣādiqeen* are two of the earliest original Shī'ah commentaries on the Qur'ān. Additionally, *Uṣūl al-Kāfī* and *Furu' al-Kāfī* are the most fundamental sources of Shī'ah narrations. The earlier editions of both "*Kāfīs*" had an inscription on the title page, reading: "According to Imām al-Mahdī, this book is *kāfī* [sufficient] for our Shī'ahs." The other two books quoted from are *Tahdheeb al-Aḥkām* and *Man Lā Yaḥdhuruhul-Faqeeh.* These, along with *Uṣūl al-Kāfī* and *Furu' al-Kāfī,* are classified among the four basic source books of Shī'ah beliefs called "*al-kutub al-arba'ah*" and are regarded as the most reliable sources of Shī'ah *fiqh.*

One could perhaps assume that these sources are obsolete and that contemporary Shī'ah scholars do not propagate such beliefs about *mut'ah.* In order to dispel such misconceptions, presented below are two citations from the work of Mullā Bāqir al-Majlisī, whom Ayatullāh Khomeini considered to be an authority on Shī'ah doctrine. It should be recalled that al-Majlisī, who died just over 300 years ago, is one of the most respected Shī'ah scholars. He wrote approximately sixty voluminous books. In several of his own writings Khomeini has referred to al-Majlisī's works. As a matter of fact, Khomeini recommended in his *Kashf al-Asrār*[273] that Shī'ahs read al-Majlisī's books, one of which deals exclusively with the merits of *mut'ah.* It has been translated into Urdu by a contemporary Shī'ah scholar named Syed Mohammad Jafar Qudsi under the title *Ijāla Ḥasna.* The following quotations are from this source:

> "The Prophet (ﷺ) said, 'One who performs *mut'ah* with a believing woman is like the one

---

[273]Page 121.

> who visits the House of God [i.e., the *Ka'bah*] seventy times.'"[274]

> "[For the] one who excels in this virtuous deed [of *mut'ah*], Allāh will raise his levels [of faith and piety]... [On the Day of Judgement] he will pass on the bridge over Hell with the speed of light... Seventy rows of angels will accompany him..., and he will enter Paradise without giving the account [of his life]. O 'Alī, one who helps a fellow Muslim brother [to contract *mut'ah*] will also receive these blessings and rewards."[275]

In conclusion is a quotation from Ayatullāh Khomeini:

> "It is permissible to engage in *mut'ah* with a fornicator woman but with a disliking in [one's] heart, especially if she is a well-known and professional fornicator. When a person contracts *mut'ah* with her, he should advise her to quit the profession of fornication."[276]

In other words, a man should first have his sexual gratification with a prostitute and then advise her to quit her profession.

Now it is left to the reader's judgement to decide if the practice of *mut'ah* is in harmony with the teachings of the Qur'ān and *sunnah* of the Prophet (ﷺ). Would such a practice establish a society based upon piety, righteousness and chastity, or rather, would it open doors to lust, lewdness and debauchery? The aforementioned citations are diametrically opposed to the Sunni position, based upon the Qur'ān and authentic prophetic *ḥadīth,* in which *mut'ah* has been totally forbidden and thus regarded as adultery and prostitution.

---

[274] *Ijāla Ḥasna,* p. 16. A forged *ḥadīth.*
[275] Ibid., p. 17.
[276] Khomeini, A.R., *Taḥreer al-Waseelah.*

For the benefit of a casual reader who could possibly have been mislead by the citations given in earlier sections, it must be reiterated that never did the Prophet (ﷺ), 'Alī, or Ja'far aṣ-Ṣādiq declare the "sanctity and blessings" of *mut'ah.* The fact is that none of the books of authentic *ḥadīth* document any of these statements; instead, in order to justify *mut'ah,* Shī'ahs have wrongfully attributed these statements to noble people and in so doing have injured the reputations of those magnanimous personalities.

Unfortunately, very few people realize the significant differences between Sunni and Shī'ah beliefs. Most Shī'ah writings and preachings revolve around the emotional issues of love for the Prophet's family members, the virtues of 'Alī, the martyrdom of al-Ḥusayn, etc. A number of people are attracted to Shī'ism because of the sensitivity and emotional nature of these issues. They do not realize that Shī'ahs have grossly misrepresented the Qur'ān, as well as distorted and forged *ḥadīths.* The concocted belief in the sanctity and merits of *mut'ah* is a classic example of such distortion.

Islāmic history has shown that wherever Shī'ahs have gained political power, legislation in favor of *mut'ah* was enforced – even at the cost of human life. During the reign of Akbar (the great Mogul emperor) in India, the chief justice, Qādhī Ya'qūb Manikpūrī, was sentenced to death for his verdict that *mut'ah* was not permissible in Islām.[277] Many people who came from the Indo-Pakistan subcontinent testified to the fact that a number of Sunni heads of state in the yet undivided India embraced Shī'ism only to indulge their lust, justifying it through the doctrine of *mut'ah.* And when prostitution was legalized by the British in India, a great many prostitutes came initially from among the Shī'ahs, perhaps practicing it as a virtuous deed.

---

[277] *Roodh-e-Kausar,* p. 102.

CONCLUSION

In closing, it is hoped that some light has been shed on the major issues which divide Shī'ahs from the main body of the Muslim *ummah.* This was a necessary undertaking since many simple and good-hearted Muslims, impressed by the enthusiastic activity and apparent sincerity of Shī'ahs, are unaware of their dangerous beliefs or assume that modern Shī'ahs have given up their radical dogmas. There has been a tendency to think of the differences between Shī'ahs and Sunnis as primarily historical and political and confined to particular *fiqh* rulings on secondary issues. Therefore, the exposure of certain distasteful facts has become imperative for the protection of both individuals and the *ummah* in general.

Almighty Allāh addressed His Messenger (ﷺ) in the Qur'ān, saying:

﴿إِنَّ الَّذِينَ فَرَّقُوا دِينَهُم وَكَانُوا شِيَعًا لَستَ مِنهُم فِي شَيءٍ إِنَّمَا أَمرُهُم إِلَى اللهِ ثُمَّ يُنَبِّئُهُم بِمَا كَانُوا يَفعَلُونَ﴾

> *"Indeed, those who have divided their religion and become sects – you are not [associated] with them in anything. Their affair is only [left] to Allāh; then He will inform them about what they used to do."*[278]

Sectarianism and deviation, even among Muslims, is a reality mentioned in several verses of the Qur'ān.[279] The Prophet (ﷺ) confirmed this, at the same time providing the key to salvation:

> *"Indeed, this nation will divide into seventy-three sects, all of them in the Fire except one." Upon being asked to specify, he (ﷺ) said,*

---

278 *Sūrah al-An'ām,* 6:159.

279 For example, see 11:118-119.

"[Except] the one following my sunnah and the way of my companions."[280]

May Allāh guide us upon the straight path of His pure and true religion and make us worthy of His approval and reward.

[280] Abū Dāwūd and others – *ṣaḥeeḥ.*

BIBLIOGRAPHY

The method of writing bibliographies in Eastern literature is somewhat different from that in Western literature. Most Eastern bibliographies record only the book's name, followed by the author. Citations of publisher and the publication year are not generally found. This is because, in the past, most books were published by their authors, and each book had only one publication.

It is additionally difficult to compile a bibliography of Shī'ah sources. When a Shī'ah publisher reprints a book, he often changes its contents. Thus, two editions of the same book by the same publisher may have two different sets of information. Consequently, a researcher may find difficulty in locating the cited pages in Shī'ah books. All of the references given in the preceding pages, however, are authentic and come from well-known Shī'ah and Sunni sources.

As a facilitation to readers, this bibliography has been annotated, and Shī'ah and Sunni sources have been duly classified.

Shī'ah Sources:

Abū 'Amr Muḥammad bin 'Abdul-'Azeez (d. 370 A.H.), *Rijāl al-Kāshī,* Bombay, India: 1317 A.H.

A source book of Shī'ah *ḥadīth* and names of Shī'ah narrators.

Aḥmad, Maqbūl, *Translation and Commentary of Qur'ān,* Maṭba'at al-Yūsufī, Delhi, India: 1929 A.D.

The very popular work of a modern Shī'ah scholar of India.

Akhtar, Hakim Zakir Husain, *Nairung Fasāḥat,* Delhi, India: Maṭba'at al-Yūsufī, 1340 A.H.

A contemporary Urdu translation of *Nahj al-Balāghah.*

al-Ardabeeli, 'Alī bin 'Īsā (d. 404 A.H.), *Kashf al-Ghummah,* Tehran, Iran: Dār al-Kutub al-Islāmiyyah, n.d.

One of the earliest original works of a Shī'ah scholar. A detailed account of the lives, deeds and sayings of the Shī'ah *imāms.*

al-'Askarī, al-Imām al-Ḥasan, *Tafseer al-'Askarī Tabriz,* Iran: 1314 A.H.

A Qur'ānic commentary by the eleventh Shī'ah *imām.*

Bābawayh, Shaykh aṣ-Ṣadūq bin Ja'far Muḥammad bin 'Alī (d. 381 A.H.), *Man Lā Yaḥdhuruhul-Faqeeh,* Najaf, Iraq: Maṭba'ah an-Najaf, 1376 A.H.

A source book considered to be one of the four original collections of Shī'ah narrations.

Ibn Abul-Ḥadeed (d. 656 A.H.), *Sharḥ Nahj al-Balāghah,* Cairo, Egypt: Dār al-Kutub Muṣṭafā al-Bābī, 1329 A.H.

One of the earliest and most respected commentaries on *Nahj al-Balāghah.*

Ibn Maysam (d. 679 A.H.), *Sharḥ Nahj al-Balāghah,* Tehran, Iran: Maṭba'ah Hydria, 1378 A.H.

One of the earliest and widely quoted commentaries of *Nahj al-Balāghah.*

Islamic Affairs, Atlanta, Georgia, USA: 172 Vine Street SW #7, Atlanta, GA 30314.

A contemporary bimonthly Shī'ah publication of the Islāmic Society of Georgia.

Jamāluddeen, Abul-Mansūr al-Ḥasan bin 'Alī bin Maṯhhar (d. 726 A.H.), *Minhāj al-Kirāmah,* Cairo, Egypt: Maktabah Dār al-'Arabiyyah, 1962.

An original work that describes and defends Shī'ah beliefs and practices and is regarded as a reference. The whole text is reproduced in Ibn Taymiyyah's *Minhāj as-Sunnah.*

al-Kāshānī, Fatḥullāh (d. 988 A.H.), *Minhāj aṣ-Ṣādiqeen,* Tehran, Iran: Dār al-Kutub al-Islāmiyyah, 1396 A.H.

One of the most famous and respected Shī'ah Qur'ānic commentaries.

al-Kāshī, Mullā Muḥsin Fā'iz, *at-Tafseer aṣ-Ṣāfī,* al-Maktabah al-Islamiyyah, Tehran, Iran: 1375 A.H.

A popular Qur'ānic commentary by a contemporary Shī'ah scholar.

al-Kashmeerī, Muḥsin, *Dabastān-e-Mazāhib,* Iran: n.d.

A book in Persian known mainly for its presentation of *Sūrah al-Wilāyah,* a chapter alleged to have removed from the Qur'ān.

Khomeini, Ayatullah (d. 1990), *al-Ḥukūmah al-Islamiyyah,* Tehran, Iran: al-Maktabah al-Islamiyyah al-Kubrā, 1981.

The most popular and well-known work of the late Shī'ah *imām* and leader of the Iranian revolution. Discusses the Shī'ah basis of the State.

Khomeini, Ayatullah, *Kashf al-Asrār,* n.d.

Presents an argument for Shī'ah doctrines, especially that of imamate.

Khomeini, Ayatullāh, *Taḥreer al-Waseelah,* Najaf, Iraq: Maṭba'ah al-Adab, 1390 A.H.

A most voluminous work on Shī'ah *fiqh* by the late Shī'ah *imām* and leader of the Iranian revolution. It consists of two volumes, consisting of 656 and 650 pages, respectively.

al-Kulaynī, Muḥammad bin Ya'qūb Abū Ja'far (d. 329 A.H.), *Furu' al-Kāfī,* Tehran, Iran: Dār al-Kutub al-Islāmiyyah, 1374 A.H.

This book is a continuation of its predecessor *Uṣūl al-Kāfī.* It contains necessary details of Shī'ah beliefs. The two books together are for Shī'ahs what al-Bukhārī and Muslim are for Sunnis.

al-Kulaynī, Muḥammad bin Ya'qūb Abū Ja'far, *Uṣūl al-Kāfī,* Tehran, Iran: Dār al-Kutub al-Islāmiyyah, 1374 A.H.

The most famous and respected collection of Shī'ah *ḥadīth.* A source book of basic Shī'ah beliefs and practices. Earlier editions carried an inscription on the title page that read: "According to Imām al-Mahdī this book is *kāfī* [sufficient] for our Shī'ahs," hence the title. It contains a total of 16,199 narrations.

al-Majlisī, Mullā Bāqir (d. 1111 A.H.), *Biḥār al-Anwār,* Lucknow, India: Maktabah Nawāl Kishore.

One of most voluminous works of al-Majlisī, it consists of 25 volumes and covers various aspects of Shī'ah beliefs, practices and history. Al-Majlisī is one of the most respected and widely quoted Shī'ah scholars, having written about 60 different books. Ayatullāh Khomeini has quoted al-Majlisī in several of his own writings, including his famous book *Kashf al-Asrār,* where he recommended al-Majlisī's books to all Shī'ahs.

al-Majlisī, Mullā Bāqir, *Ḥaqq al-Yaqeen,* Lucknow, India: Maktabah Nawāl Kishore, 1303 A.H.

Another classical work of al-Majlisī. Khomeini also made a special recommendation about this work in his *Kashf al-Asrār.*

al-Majlisī, Mullā Bāqir, *Ḥayāt al-Qulūb,* Lucknow, India: Maktabah Nawāl Kishore, 1303 A.H.

A voluminous work dealing mainly with the virtues and teachings of the Shī'ah *imāms.*

al-Majlisī, Mullā Bāqir, *Jalāl al-'Ayūn,* Lucknow, India: Maktabah Nawāl Kishore.

Another voluminous work dealing mainly with the history of the Prophet (ﷺ) and the Shī'ah *imāms.*

Qudsi, Syed M. Jafar, *Ijāla Ḥasna,* Lahore, Pakistan: Imamia General Book Agency, n.d.

An Urdu translation of Mullā Bāqir al-Majlisī's book on *mut'ah.* Several different editions of the book have been published in India and Pakistan.

al-Qummī, 'Alī bin Ibrāheem (d. 381 A.H.), *Tafseer al-Qummī,* Najaf, Iraq: Maṭba'ah an-Najaf, 1386 A.H.

Regarded as the oldest and most respected Shī'ah Qur'ānic commentary.

ar-Rāzī, Syed Sharīf (d. 404 A.H.), *Nahj al-Balāghah,* Cairo, Egypt: Maṭba'ah ar-Raḥmāniyyah (also Beirut, Lebanon: Maṭba'ah Maḥmasī), n.d.

A compilation of 'Alī's sermons. A popular Shī'ah book, although history does not support its reliability.

Rizvi, S., *Imāmate,* Tehran, Iran: P.O. Box 2245.

A recent publication that summarizes and defends the Shī'ah belief in imamate.

Shoostry, Noorullah (d. 1019 A.H.), *Iḥqāq al-Ḥaqq,* Tehran, Iran: Maṭba'ah al-Islamiyyah, 1391 A.H.

A classical work by the great Shī'ah scholar of the Mogul period in India.

aṭ-Ṭabarsī, Aḥmad bin 'Alī (d. 548 A.H.), *Al-Iḥtijāj 'alā Ahl al-Lajāj,* Tehran, Iran: Maṭba'ah al-Islamiyyah, 1302 A.H.

A reference for Shī'ah doctrines and practices.

aṭ-Ṭabarsī, Mirzā Ḥusayn bin Muḥammad Taqī an-Nūrī (d. 1320 A.H.), *Faṣl al-Khiṭāb fī Ithbāt Taḥreef Kitāb Rabb al-Arbāb,* Tehran, Iran: 1298 A.H.

The work of a contemporary Shī'ah scholar citing numerous quotations of earlier Shī'ah writers asserting the unreliability of the existing Qur'ān.

aṭ-Ṭabarsī, Mirzā Ḥusayn bin Muḥammad Taqī an-Nūrī, *Raddu Ba'dhish-Shubuhāti 'an Faṣl al-Khiṭāb fī Ithbāt Taḥreef Kitāb Rabb al-Arbāb,* Tehran, Iran: 1318 A.H.

The book discusses and refutes objections raised by contemporary Shī'ah scholars about the author's former book which tries to prove the unreliability of the existing Qur'ān.

aṭ-Ṭūsī, Shaykh Abū Ja'far (d. 460 A.H.), *Tahdheeb al-Aḥkām,* Tehran, Iran: Dār al-Kutub al-Islāmiyyah, n.d.

A source book considered to be one of the four original collections of Shī'ah *ḥadīth.*

Ya'qūb, Aḥmad bin Abī Ya'qūb (d. 256 A.H.), *Tareekh al-Ya'qūbī,* Beirut, Lebanon: Maktabah Dār aṣ-Ṣadr, 1392 A.H.

One of the earliest Shī'ah sources of history.

Sunni Sources:

al-'Abbāsī, Maḥmūd Aḥmad, *Khilāfat Mu'āwiyah and Yazeed,* Karachi, Pakistan: Sultan Hasan & Sons, 1962.

A comprehensive and objective work on the history of al-Ḥusayn's martyrdom at Karbala.

Abū Dāwūd, Sulaymān (d. 275 A.H.), *Sunan Abī Dāwūd,* Cairo, Egypt: Maktabah Anṣār as-Sunnah, 1949.

Classified as one of six most authentic and original sources of Sunni *ḥadīth* known as the *Ṣiḥāḥ as-Sittah.* Contains 4,800 *ḥadīths.*

Anas, Mālik (d. 179 A.H.), *al-Muwaṭṭa',* Cairo, Egypt: Maktabah Muṣṭafā al-Bābī, 1961.

One of the earliest collection of *ḥadīths* and classified as one of the most reliable. Contains 1,720 *ḥadīths.*

al-Bukhārī, Muḥammad bin Ismā'eel (d. 256 A.H.), *Ṣaḥeeḥ al-Bukhārī,* Cairo, Egypt: Maktabah Muṣṭafā al-Bābī, 1959.

The most authentic Sunni collection of *ḥadīths.* Contains 7,563 *ḥadīths.*

Ibn Abī Shaybah, Abū Bakr, *'Ilal Ibn Abī Shaybah,* Multan, Pakistan: Maṭba'ah Iqbāl, 1340 A.H.

A collection of *ḥadīths* with a hidden defect by an early Sunni scholar.

Ibn Ḥanbal, Aḥmad, *Al-Musnad,* Cairo, Egypt: 1313 A.H.

A well-known collection of *ḥadīths* by Imām Aḥmad.

Ibn al-Jawzī, Jamāluddeen, *'Umar bin al-Khaṭṭāb,* Cairo, Egypt: Maktabah Muḥammad Sabiḥ, n.d.

A comprehensive and reliable book on the life of the second caliph.

Ibn Katheer, Ismā'eel 'Imāduddeen (d. 774 A.H.), *al-Bidāyah wan-Nihāyah,* Beirut, Lebanon: Maktabah al-Ma'ārif, 1977.

A classical and respected history.

Ibn Katheer, Ismā'eel 'Imāduddeen, *Tafseer Ibn Katheer,* Karachi, Pakistan: Noor Mohammad Publishers.

A voluminous and respected commentary on the Qur'ān.

Ibn Sa'd, Muḥammad (d. 260 A.H.), *Ṭabaqāt Ibn Sa'd,* Beirut, Lebanon: Dār aṣ-Ṣadr, 1968.

One of the earliest references on Islāmic history.

Ibn Taymiyyah (d. 748 A.H.), *Minhāj as-Sunnah,* Cairo, Egypt: Maktabah Dār al-'Arabiyyah, 1962.

A comprehensive, critical analysis of Shī'ah beliefs and practices.

Ikrām, Shaykh Muḥammad, *Roodh-e-Kausar,* Lahore, Pakistan: Ferooz Sons, 1958.

A classical Urdu work used as a university textbook.

al-Makkī, Ibn Ḥajr (d. 973 A.H.), *aṣ-Ṣawā'iq al-Muḥarriqah,* Cairo, Egypt: Maktabah al-Qāhirah, 1965.

A classical work dealing with innovations in Islām.

Muslehuddin, M., *Muta,* Lahore, Pakistan: Islamic Publication Ltd., 1974.

A contemporary book discussing the illegality of *mut'ah* according to the Qur'ān and *sunnah.*

Muslim, Ibn al-Ḥajjāj (d. 261 A.H.), *Ṣaḥeeḥ Muslim,* Delhi, India: aṣ-Ṣaḥ al-Mujtabai, 1349 A.H.

Regarded as the second most authentic collection of Sunni *ḥadīths.* Contains over 3,000 *ḥadīths.*

an-Nasā'ī, 'Abdur-Raḥmān Aḥmad (d. 303 A.H.), *Sunan an-Nasā'ī,* Cairo, Egypt: Maktabah Muṣṭafā al-Bābī, 1964.

One of the *Ṣiḥāḥ as-Sittah.*

aṭ-Ṭabarī, Ibn Jareer (d. 310 A.H.), *Tareekh aṭ-Ṭabarī,* Dār al-Ma'ārif, 1962.

A comprehensive work of Muslim history which also presents the Shī'ah perspective.

aṭ-Ṭabarī, al-Muḥibb (d. 694 A.H.), *ar-Riyādh an-Nathirah,* Cairo, Egypt: Maktabah Muṣṭafā al-Bābī, 1327 A.H.

A classical work of early Muslim history.

at-Tabrīzī, Waliyyudeen al-Khaṭeeb (d. 737 A.H.), *Mishkāt al-Maṣābīḥ,* Lahore, Pakistan: The Book House.

A respected compilation of *ḥadīths* mostly from *Ṣiḥāḥ as-Sittah.*

at-Tirmidhī, Muḥammad bin 'Īsā (d. 279 A.H.), *Jāmi'at-Tirmidhī* (also called *Sunan at-Tirmidhī*), Cairo, Egypt: Maktabah Muṣṭafā al-Bābī, 1963.

Classified as one of the *Ṣiḥāḥ as-Sittah.* Contains 2,028 *ḥadīths.*

Other Sources:

Gibbs, H. A. R. and Kramer, J. H., *Shorter Encyclopaedia of Islam,* Leiden: J. R. Brill, 1961 (also Ithaca, N.Y., USA: Cornell University Press, 1953).